"Joel Zeff is a multifaceted motivator. He wears many hats: teacher, coach, cheerleader, and comedian. He is funny. *Make the Right Choice*'s wisdom can prompt you to pause, reflect on life's priorities, and inspire personal growth."

—Kelli Finglass
Director, Dallas Cowboys Cheerleaders; Star and Executive Producer,
Dallas Cowboys Cheerleaders: Making the Team

Praise for *Make the Right Choice*

"Magicians spend years perfecting the art of TA DA. Kids earn a TA DA with each baby step. *Make the Right Choice* is a "just right" approach to discover your TA DA, in achievable, actionable steps. Zeff's storytelling style will reach your mind, heart, and funny bone. You'll laugh your way to making a difference in your leadership, communication, and the choices you make every day. That is the real magic of Joel Zeff."

—Kelly McCutcheon
Group Director of Training and Development, Whataburger

"Having known Joel Zeff for years and witnessed his electrifying presentations to both nonprofits and clients, I can confidently say that *Make the Right Choice* has been a cornerstone in understanding how to create a positive and productive work environment. His unique blend of humor and wisdom has always resonated with me, helping to transform my approach to workplace challenges. And now, TA DA! Joel introduces a new and improved edition of his book, enhancing the already invaluable advice with even more insights and practical tips. If you thought the original was a game changer, this updated version will inspire anyone who reads it to make the right choices in their professional life, elevating their work experience to new heights of enjoyment and innovation!"

—Richard Honiball
EVP, Global Chief Merchandising & Marketing Officer;
Adjunct Instructor, George Mason University;
Retail Executive with Navy Exchange, JC Penney, Haggar Clothing

"Joel's book *Make the Right Choice* shares so many great tools and advice to be successful. I really resonated with this book, and I know it will be a powerful tool for people to utilize in their own lives!"

—Carly Patterson
Olympic Gold Medalist; Member, USA Gymnastics Hall of Fame

JOEL ZEFF

FULLY REVISED AND UPDATED WITH THE SPIRIT OF 'TA DA!'

MAKE THE RIGHT CHOICE

LEAD WITH PASSION, ELEVATE YOUR TEAM, AND UNLEASH THE FUN AT WORK

WILEY

Published by John Wiley & Sons, Inc., Hoboken, New Jersey.
Published simultaneously in Canada.

For general information on our other products and services or for technical support, please contact our Customer Care Department within the United States at (800) 762-2974, outside the United States at (317) 572-3993 or fax (317) 572-4002.

Wiley also publishes its books in a variety of electronic formats. Some content that appears in print may not be available in electronic formats. For more information about Wiley products, visit our web site at www.wiley.com.

Library of Congress Cataloging-in-Publication Data

Names: Zeff, Joel, author.
Title: Make the right choice : lead with passion, elevate your team, and unleash the fun at work / Joel Zeff.
Description: Hoboken, New Jersey : Wiley, [2025] | Includes index.
Identifiers: LCCN 2024031221 (print) | LCCN 2024031222 (ebook) | ISBN 9781394278954 (hardback) | ISBN 9781394278978 (adobe pdf) | ISBN 9781394278961 (epub)
Subjects: LCSH: Quality of work life. | Choice (Psychology) | Change (Psychology) | Resilience (Personality trait) | Creative ability in business.
Classification: LCC HD6955 .Z44 2025 (print) | LCC HD6955 (ebook) | DDC 306.3—dc23/eng/20240801
LC record available at https://lccn.loc.gov/2024031221
LC ebook record available at https://lccn.loc.gov/2024031222

Cover Design: Paul McCarthy
SKY10085502_091924

For Isabella and Zander to help them make the right choices in life.

And for Susan, who helps me make the right choices each day.

And for every audience member who listened, laughed, engaged, applauded, and smiled.

And especially for those awesome audience members who joined me on stage.

Huge TA DA!

Contents

Contents

Preface

It is, in fact, nothing short of a miracle that the modern methods of instruction have not entirely strangled the holy curiosity of inquiry.

—Albert Einstein

Learning is not attained by chance; it must be sought for with ardor and attended to with diligence.

—Abigail Adams

This book is not for Dumb Ass Managers (D.A.M.s). They refuse to turn away from their presentations of upside-down triangles and convoluted mission statements; they certainly do not listen to you; and they are too busy micromanaging to read a book. They only learn from another D.A.M.

Take a moment to watch and study a D.A.M. in their natural habitat. Look down the hall at the cubicle on the right; the D.A.M. is focused on something that doesn't matter while also trying to convince someone that they had communicated a key detail (they didn't) about an expense to a vendor that caused confusion and mayhem. There is another D.A.M. in their vice president's office, taking credit for a success that had nothing to do with them. Or maybe you are attending a conference and you see a D.A.M. near the coffee station. They tend to circle near blueberry muffins. They probably wouldn't notice you watching them. The D.A.M. stuffs their face with a muffin, staring at their phone and answering emails about fungibles.[1]

Every so often, the D.A.M. must feed. The D.A.M. feeds on other team members after a larger and stronger D.A.M. requires quarterly performance improvements.

A typical D.A.M. wants success. They want their employees to have passion and creativity. They want their team to produce results. And then the D.A.M. clubs them like baby seals.

Nope, this is not a book for a D.A.M. This is a book for the baby seals. Unlike real baby seals, which are innocent and helpless, you can choose to be something else. You can choose to be a polar bear. You can choose to be anything you want. It is always your choice.

You can choose to be happy, passionate, creative, and energetic. You can choose to be open and flexible to change and to create opportunity and positive support. You can choose to help those around you be successful. You can choose to be in the moment and stay in the game. This is a book for the baby seals and polar bears to make those choices. This is even a book for the people who use words such as "fungible." I just cannot help a D.A.M. because they refuse to listen, refuse to learn something new, and refuse to support their team. They think they are always right. I just do not have that kind of power.

I have met and worked with plenty of D.A.M.s over the years. Since 1997, I have spoken at more than 2,500 events for almost every industry.[2] I invite audience members to come on stage and perform improvisation exercises with me to learn about communication, teamwork, change, leadership, innovation, accountability, and fun. Thousands of volunteers have jumped onstage with me over the years: CEOs, vice presidents, entry-level employees, interns, students, middle managers, upper managers, lower managers, managers of managers, and their employees who build, manufacture, distribute, sell, market, buy, and generally do all the work.

Every time I speak and perform, I learn something new about how we communicate and work together. By watching thousands of people from all walks of life play these improvisation games, I have noticed the choices that make them successful. I also noticed the choices that lead to disappointing results.

This book is a combination of what improvisation taught me about business and life, and what the thousands of volunteers have taught me over the years. By playing the improvisation exercises with so many different companies, organizations, and corporate cultures, I feel like an anthropologist studying wild animals in their natural habitat.

When I started speaking, I never sat down and wrote out my messages. My early clients would ask for an outline of my presentation, and I would have to tell them there wasn't one. I played the improvisation games and spoke from the heart. When I delivered a message I liked, I would make a mental note to incorporate that thought into my next presentation. My keynote continually evolved, fueled by experience and observation. It continues to evolve even today.

In the Beginning, I Was a Reporter. I Didn't Even Know People Spoke for a Living

I started my career as a journalist. I then moved into public relations, advertising, and marketing, primarily for technology and telecommunications companies. In 1994, I started my own consulting business, helping companies with their public relations and marketing. The year before, in 1993, I began performing improvisational comedy professionally at a theater in Dallas, Texas. I performed more than 3,500 shows with the same improvisation comedy troupe. I worked in two different worlds. In one world, I performed improvisational comedy. In the other world, I worked in public relations, advertising, and marketing. I realized the skills that made each successful were quite similar. And I found a way to combine the two worlds.

I knew that improvisation was originally used as a teaching tool, but I never thought about using the games in a business environment. One day, a client, who knew what I did on the weekend with the improvisation group, invited me to a meeting. The client was having a retreat and asked whether I could play some of the improvisation games with the executives. Another performer and I played a dozen or so games with the group. The small audience was made up of executive vice presidents from a technology firm. They loved the games, and a light bulb started flickering above my head. Pretty soon, more clients were asking me to speak. I put together some very raw, inexpensive, and strange promotional materials, and my career as a speaker began. At the time, I had no idea people even spoke for a living.

My experience with improvisation was my foundation for my presentations. When I started, I was just focused on the entertainment aspect of the games and a few of the messages that I picked up while studying and performing. Very quickly, I realized that improvisation forced the participants to make the right choices for success. I observed how employees and managers played the games and interacted with each other. It was very apparent that the games were a microcosm of how we communicated and functioned as a team. The same choices the volunteers made to achieve success in the improvisation games were the ones required at their jobs.

Every Employee and Manager Wants to Have Fun

I saw countless employees and managers from different levels, backgrounds, nationalities, and industries make the same choices. It was very enlightening. I also discovered how creative, energetic, passionate, and fun we all are, given the right opportunity and the right positive environment. The sad part is that too many companies fail to provide the opportunity and positive support needed. I have walked into too many meetings that had the same energy as the waiting room where you get your tires rotated. There was no energy or passion. Many of my clients would tell me their groups were boring, uninterested in participating, unresponsive, cynical, or "not very creative." Within seconds of walking on stage, I had those same groups laughing, creating energy, and having fun. They volunteered. They participated. Most importantly, they learned how to unleash their creativity, communicate effectively, and work together more successfully.

The one constant I quickly discovered was that *we are all creative*. And we all want to have fun. Sometimes, all we need is the right opportunity, the right leader, and the right positive support.

Improvisation is the tool I use to make audiences laugh and think. By creating an entertaining atmosphere, the audiences are more open to the messages. More importantly, they retain the message. My presentations are not about teaching participants the art of improvisation. I use improvisation as my foundation and filter the lessons through my vision and business experience. The games allow the audience to easily see, participate, and understand my messages about teamwork, creativity, and communication. The choices the employees and managers make playing the games are equally part of my presentation's foundation. The volunteers are just as much a part of this book as the improvisation games.

Improvisation is very special to me. You can learn quite a bit about a person by watching them play the games. Some of the questions I can answer after observing audience members participate in the exercises are:

- Who is open and flexible to change?
- Who is patient and understanding?
- Who is supportive and helpful?

- Who is creative?
- Who is a leader?
- Who helps others achieve success?
- Who works successfully in a team environment?

We Have to Take Responsibility and Make the Right Choice

Each chapter in this book will discuss a specific choice that we can each make to achieve more success in our communication, teamwork, and leadership goals. I will also give ideas and tips on becoming a better leader and teammate; learning to be more innovative; communicating more effectively; attaining more success as an employee or manager; and living a more passionate, energized, and happier life.[3]

This book has the same spirit as my presentations. I include plenty of great messages and ideas. And I promise each chapter will have plenty of quality fun—equal to a generous assortment of cupcake sprinkles, balloons, and balls that light up when they bounce. And there might even be just a small dash of irreverence. My goal is for each chapter to inform and amuse. You might even giggle. I hope you will laugh. You work hard. You deserve to laugh and have fun. We all do.

This book is not a long, boring treatise on the intricacies of business. These are not earth-shattering revelations. I have seen too many books that break down communication or creativity into one long scientific and sociological thesis that forgets to inspire, educate, motivate, or entertain. These messages are simple, straightforward choices that were taught to us by our parents and grandparents. Sometimes, though, we get so caught up in our conference calls, emails, reports, deadlines, PowerPoint presentations, and to-do lists that we forget some of these key messages that make us more productive, creative, effective, and happy. We have to relearn. And then we have to relearn again.

We are busy people. We try to do so many things at once that we sometimes forget the little things that allow us to do the big things successfully. This book focuses on the little things: simple choices that we can all make to be more successful and happier.

Improvisation is an art. It is an art that teaches and entertains. I continue to be amazed by the volunteers who come on stage. And I continue to learn something new every time I speak and perform. Thank you for allowing me to share my passion with you. I hope this book will make you think. I also hope I make you smile along the way.

This book is also about whimsy, silliness, and fun. The inventor of improvisation believed in learning during play. She believed in playing improvisation games to understand important acting concepts. My guiding light is always the pursuit of fun and laughter.

I hope you have fun reading this book. I hope you enjoy the stories and humor as I discuss my messages on leadership, teamwork, communication, change, and more.

As you read this book, I want you to think about socks. Yep, socks. Years ago, an attendee at a jeweler's conference bestowed a gift of socks to me with a board member's face on them. She gave socks with my face on them to the board member. She wanted to commemorate the fun the board member and I had when we appeared on stage. To me, the socks represent the importance of silliness and whimsy.

The board member became president of the organization. As the emcee, I wore the socks with his face on them on stage as a fun joke. Two years later, a new president led the organization. His wife bought socks with his face and gave them to me. And I wore them on stage. The silliness spread. One pair of socks started something.

You would think the sock story would end here. Nope. Two years later, the organization appointed their first woman president. And they bought socks for me with her face emblazoned on them. And I wore them on stage. Three presidents with face socks. This would be great place for the story to end. Nope.

I am on a Zoom call with a financial client. As we discussed their event, one of the attendees posed a question: "Can we do the sock bit at the event?"

"What sock bit?" I replied.

The client had seen a video from the jeweler's event. I explained it was an inside joke with this client and how the joke had transpired over the years. Undeterred, they wanted the sock bit. I relented, wondering how this inside joke had now jumped to another client. At the event, the financial audience loved the sock bit as I paraded on stage with their leader's face on my socks.

Did the sock bit continue? Yep. A new president was sworn in to the jeweler's organization. This time, I explained to the audience the entire story of the sock bit, showing photos, and explaining how it had jumped to another client. I asked the sound person to play the music from *2001: A Space Odyssey* as I unveiled the socks. The crowd loved it.

I have now worn socks with five people's face on them from two different organizations. It all started with an attendee and a fun idea. You never know where fun and silliness will take you. You have to be open to the idea of fun and sometimes take a chance in creating that fun.

We all crave connection and fun. Those face socks represent that connection. And I hope the stories and messages in this book will inspire you to connect with your team. Who knows, you may even create a face sock tradition.

Take care, and I wish you continued success. I hope to see you at your next meeting. I will be the one on stage wearing socks with someone's face on them. Also, try to save me a blueberry muffin from the D.A.M.

Quick Ideas

At the end of most of the chapters, I offer some quick ideas to help you in your quest in making the right choices. Since this is the preface, the only idea I have to offer is to read the rest of this book. To help you, here are a few ideas on where and when to read this book:

- Read this book on airplanes, while standing in line, waiting for the doctor, or any place in public. Laugh very loud. When someone asks you what you are laughing about, hold the book up and proclaim, "This is one damn good book." When they ask the author's name, be sure to spell my name. Otherwise, everyone will end up calling me "Jeff."

- Read this book in the bathroom. I have spent countless hours scientifically researching the length of each chapter, reading speed of an average adult, and the amount of time spent in the bathroom during a normal break, and I can assure you it's a perfect fit.

- Read this book at work. Take a few minutes from scrolling Instagram, Tinder, and Poshmark or playing a game on your phone and read a chapter.

- Read this book at a conference during any panel or Q&A session. Seriously, has anyone gained knowledge or inspiration from watching a panel discussion?

- Read this book during non-video conference calls with more than three people on the call. Conference calls with more than three people are slightly less productive than the average panda bear.

- Read this book while eating a blueberry muffin.

Chapter 1

The Secrets of TA DA: Celebrating Moments to Fuel Our Passion

Success is not the key to happiness. Happiness is the key to success. If you love what you are doing, you will be successful.

—Albert Schweitzer

Love life, engage in it, give it all you've got. Love it with a passion, because life truly does give back, many times over, what you put into it.

—Maya Angelou

I always start my keynote presentations with a TA DA! The audience stands up. We count to three, stretch our hands high in the air, and yell out, "TA DA!" People laugh. Some audience members applaud. And then we do it again. We all need a TA DA.[1]

After more than 2,500 events, I have seen accountants, lawyers, IT professionals, salespeople, maintenance supervisors, truck drivers, surgeons, teachers, front-line workers, and everyone else yell, "TA DA!" We can all agree that everyone likes positive support and appreciation. And that is the secret of TA DA. We all want to "TA DA!" We just don't admit it.

Before I ask the audience to stand and yell out TA DA, I tell a story. We were all kids (I have no scientific evidence of this; I am just going on assumption). We built block towers and called them spaceships. We rode a bike for the first time. We used the bathroom by ourselves for the first time. We tied our shoes. We drew orange unicorns, purple and red trees, and eight-legged dogs/cats/whales. And after each glorious achievement, someone yelled, "TA DA!"

The TA DA gave us confidence as children. The positive reinforcement made us want to do the action again. We announced to the world and to ourselves that we accomplished something. As we aged, we stopped giving ourselves a TA DA. We rarely received a TA DA from the people around us. Accomplishments became routine. We limited our celebrations. Sure, once a year we gave out pointy glass awards to a few people in the company. That should make you sad.

The TA DA is about celebrating moments. We all do great things for our customers, team, and partners each day. Moments that deserve celebration.

One of the cool things about my job is that I get a round of applause. How lucky is that? I do my job; I get a round of applause. Every time. Most people do not have a job where they get a round of applause. Wouldn't it be great if a colleague started the day by giving you a round of applause for managing, distributing, fixing, manufacturing, or (insert job title or what you do)?

If someone is not going to give you a round of applause, give it to yourself when you show up for work. People may look at you strangely. Just look right back, and keep giving yourself applause. You deserve it. We all do. Applause builds confidence. Applause gives us fuel to reach our goals, to be a better leader and teammate, to be a better communicator, and to find success.

We all work hard. And we still need a TA DA because it fulfills our basic needs (after food, water, shelter, clothing, Wi-Fi, and Netflix).

Here is my breakdown of the purpose and reasoning behind the TA DA. To me, there are five secrets of TA DA:

1. We want to feel appreciated.

Appreciation is our fuel. We desire more than a paycheck to be fulfilled and rewarded. During my presentations, I ask audience volunteers to come to the stage and perform an improvisation game. The more applause and laughter they receive from the audience, the more they do. We all want appreciation from our team, customers, and managers. And we also want appreciation from ourselves. That is the first secret of TA DA. We are announcing to the world that we appreciate ourselves.

2. We want to be respected.

Giving someone recognition and appreciation means giving respect. We have worked hard, sacrificed, faced challenges, and overcome obstacles. Sure, we want the appreciation. We also want respect. And if standing up, hands in the air, and yelling "TA DA" does not give you respect, I don't know what will.

3. We want to be recognized.

Recognition is the third secret of the TA DA. We want someone to notice that we have accomplished something. We want people to pay attention. We want someone to react to our TA DA. We want to stand in the crowd and yell out TA DA so that everyone will notice.

4. We want to be triumphant.

There is a pomp and circumstance to the TA DA. You stand up, arms raised, and yell it out. We are sounding our horn of success. We have finished a report, project, plan, or PowerPoint presentation with an upside-down triangle and interlocking circles. We have defeated the dragon. We want to yell from a mountain top. We want to beat our chests and scream to the world. Since decorum is usually in order, the TA DA serves this purpose without someone taking you to jail.

5. We want a surprise.

When the magician finishes his illusion, there is gusto, a flourish, and a TA DA. We want to be surprised that the tiger/assistant/plane/Statue of Liberty/seven of hearts has reappeared.[2] The TA DA is always a surprise. You never know when the need bubbles up in you. You never know what really deserves a TA DA. The surprise makes the TA DA even more exciting.

There is no right or wrong way to TA DA. It can be spontaneous. It can be organized. The spirit of TA DA is what matters. Here are four recent ideas I have come across to show appreciation and spread the spirit of TA DA:

1. Tip of the Hat

To me, one of the best ways to show appreciation is in front of the whole team or group. Even better is when the positive support is spontaneous. At a recent event for an insurance company, the host started the program with a segment called "Tip of the Hat." The rules were simple. He put a four-minute timer on the screen. During that time, anyone could stand and appreciate, thank, and recognize another team member or group. The positive support, words of appreciation, and applause started the meeting with a huge TA DA. They start all their big meetings this way.

2. Appreciation Board

This is a variation of "Tip of the Hat." I have recently seen this idea twice. There is a designated "appreciation board"

Make the Right Choice

outside (or inside) the meeting room. Attendees can write and post appreciation notes to team members, managers, or leaders during the conference. During breaks, everyone is reading the posted notes or writing new ones. The best part is reading a few of the notes at the close of the event. You do not have to do this at a meeting. Put an appreciation board in the break room, in the reception area, bathroom, or conference room.

3. LOVE Letters

There are a thousand different ways to create a more organized appreciation program. A credit union in Houston has a cool program called "Letters Outlining Valuable Experiences" (LOVE). The program is simple:

1. Members or associates send a little love through an appreciation email, phone call, letter, or other medium.

2. Letters are collected each month and reviewed. A monthly MVP is selected and given a traveling trophy and a certificate.

3. Monthly winners are then considered for annual awards and prizes.

4. Video Testimonials

At a recent leadership event, the client played videos before each segment or speaker, called "How ____ inspires me." Team members from each leader's location would talk about how the person inspired them, mentored them, or displayed incredible leadership. These videos were powerful, emotional, and inspiring. The video was a simple idea that delivered powerful results. The videos (which were recorded on a phone) were authentic and from the heart.

It is easy to put the TA DA into practice. Every day when you go home, think about all the people you met. Did you give appreciation and positive support to those who deserved it? Did you say thank you? If you didn't, then tomorrow send a note, email, or letter. Give them a call. See them in the hall and say thank you. There is no expiration date on a thank you.

You don't need a budget for a TA DA. You don't need permission. You don't have to do anything, really. You just stand up, put your hands in the air, and yell, "TA DA!" Go ahead. You deserve it.

TA DA!

Chapter 2

The Story of Losing My Job and a Magic Harmonica

The way I see it, if you want the rainbow, you gotta put up with the rain.

—Dolly Parton

I've been absolutely terrified every moment of my life—and I've never let it keep me from doing a single thing I wanted to do.

—Georgia O'Keefe

I lost my job in 1991. Most of us will receive the "come clean out your desk and here is your severance check" phone call at some point in our careers. I received that call on a Sunday at the end of 1991. I had no idea that in a few hours a magic harmonica would save me.

Nobody wants to receive that phone call. Sitting on my couch in a one-bedroom apartment with little other furniture, I could not believe I had just lost my job. Six months before the phone call, I had moved to Texas to work as a reporter for the *Dallas Times Herald*. And now the newspaper was closing and would print the last issue the following day. Every employee of the paper was now joining the unemployed.

The call ended. Something strange happened. I experienced relief and not anger (insert screeching sound). Yep, I was elated. Weight lifted from my shoulders. To be honest, the job was overflowing with challenges. It did not take long after I joined the paper to realize I had jumped on board the *Titanic* right as it was leaving the dock. I can still hear the horn and someone yelling, "All aboard!" The *Titanic* passengers had no idea they were on a ship that would hit an iceberg. I, however, was fully aware I was on the newspaper *Titanic*. Six months after I moved to Dallas, the newspaper had hit the iceberg.[1]

After the call, I took a breath. I thought about losing my job. Like many, I was not happy at my job. Still, it was a job. Now what? I thought about what I was going to do. Would I have to move to another city? How do I pay rent? How will this affect my career? Should I stop for lunch before going to clean out my desk or is that rude? What are the protocols for cleaning out your desk on a Sunday?

Walking out my door to head to the newsroom to clean out my desk, I grabbed my harmonica. At that moment, I did not think it was a magical instrument. I still have no idea why I put the harmonica in my pocket. This was not a normal activity. Full disclosure: I am tone deaf. I have no musical ability. I cannot really play the harmonica. I can make some semblance of sound that does not make a cat or baby wail.

I had purchased the harmonica in college. I attended a lecture and walked out with a new harmonica. I am guessing the guest speaker played the harmonica. I have no memory of the speaker. Someone was selling harmonicas, and I had some extra cash in my pocket. It made sense at the time. Who knew that this harmonica was magical or would change my life?

I always say that the day I lost my job as a newspaper reporter was one of the best days of my life.[2] Walking into the newsroom, I noticed everyone experiencing a range of emotions: sadness, anger, confusion, defeat. To me, I just felt relief. I saw this day as opportunity and a new beginning.

As everyone cleaned out their desk and grabbed everything that was not bolted to the wall, I found myself on the back loading dock where the media covering the paper's demise had assembled. The closing of a daily newspaper was a big deal in 1991. Television and news radio reporters gathered to cover the end. I surveyed the scene. I never thought, "Hey, I should go see who is hanging out on the back loading dock and play the harmonica for them." It just happened. I took out my magic harmonica and poorly played a blues note. "Da-dana-dun-dun." The lyrics went something like this: "I lost my job. I got no money . . . I just moved to Dallas. The newspaper closed. I have no money. I got the newspaper blues." This went on for a few minutes.[3]

The next part is just like a movie. Someone grabbed my elbow and told me to stop. I have no idea who said those words. I have lost that memory. I do remember them saying, "You will never work in this town again." True story. I cannot believe someone said that to me—and meant it! It was just like a film noir movie.

I ended up on two local television newscasts, had my photo in the Fort Worth Star Telegram, and the story of me playing the harmonica after losing my job was picked up nationally. Remember, this is before social media. People from around the country would call me and ask, "Did I see you play the harmonica on the news?" Yep.

That evening, colleagues gathered to mourn the newspaper's ending. We watched the local news broadcast. And there I am playing the harmonica. I could not believe it. A 112-year-old paper closed, and there is a 23-year-old idiot playing the harmonica. It was silly. And for a moment, I forgot the negativity and doubt about losing my job.

The magic harmonica forced me to choose my attitude. I chose how I reacted to change and disruption.

The Story of Losing My Job and a Magic Harmonica

It is always a tough day when you lose your job. The magic harmonica taught me there is always something else out there. I had a desire that I was ignoring. A path I was not taking.

That magic harmonica (which I still have) taught me to embrace change and disruption. It taught me that fun and whimsy are part of my life. It taught me to stay in the game and create opportunity. Soon after the *Herald* closed, I started doing stand up and improvisational comedy. I auditioned and was asked to join an improvisational comedy troupe. Years later, I would use those skills as the foundation for my keynote speaking and emcee business. And that led me to writing this book. All because of a magic harmonica.

I did not understand all the gifts from the magic harmonica in that moment. After reflection, I think there are seven gifts. These gifts do not include the three-hole punch, stapler, and dictionary that I took from the *Herald*. Yes, I still have all three. Take my advice, when in doubt, grab the three-hole punch.

1. Reduce the Stress

Losing your job is a huge life event. It causes stress. The magic harmonica allowed me to take a step back during the moment of chaos and disruption. Playing the magic harmonica reduced my stress. It forced me to embrace my silliness. It made me smile and remember what was truly important.

2. Create Confidence

Trust your abilities. Trust your skills. Yes, I lost my job. I did not lose my skills and abilities. Playing the magic harmonica in front of my colleagues and the news media exuded confidence. Remember, I have no musical ability. The cool thing about the harmonica instrument is you can fake it for a few seconds and people will think you have skills. This is another reason that the harmonica is magical. Young twenty-something unemployed man with no musical ability plays the harmonica in front of colleagues and the assembled media is the definition of confidence. Any action that creates confidence will build more confidence. It is a defining moment. This is who I am.

3. Embrace Change and Disruption

Change and disruption can be scary. We do not know what happens next. Embrace the unknown. Losing your job forces you to change course. The new direction has the potential to be more fulfilling and rewarding. I loved being a journalist. I love being a keynote speaker more.

4. Focus on the Moment

Playing the magic harmonica forced me to focus and be in the moment. I did not know the moment would become a driving force in my career. Being in the moment will always produce results.

5. Take a Risk

Sometimes you just take the leap. You throw yourself out there. Most people would never play harmonica and make up a song in front of television cameras. And that is why two local broadcasts used the footage and there was a photo in the newspaper. They expect employees who just lost their job to be angry, sad, and confused. They do not expect someone to play the "Newspaper Blues."

6. Be Who You Are

My humor is my superpower. It gives me strength. It gets me out of tough situations. It comforts me. What is your superpower? Are you utilizing that power to create a fulfilling and rewarding career? The moment with the magic harmonica (and the reality that I had quite a bit of free time now) gave me the confidence to start performing stand-up comedy. Stand-up led me to improvisation. And improv led me to speaking.

7. Choose Your Attitude

Most change is out of our control. We can only control how we react to change. I did not control the newspaper closing. I did not control that I lost my job. I only controlled how I reacted to the situation. The magic harmonica made me choose my attitude. Instead of being upset, angry, sad, dejected, and every negative emotion, I chose to be positive, upbeat, and hopeful. I truly believed this was an opportunity. I did not want the powers in charge of closing the newspaper to beat me. I was going to choose my attitude.[4]

I often wonder what would have happened if I did not lose my job that day. How long would I have continued as a journalist? Would I have moved to another reporting job? Would I have ever become a keynote speaker? Would I have written this book? And if I did not write this book you would still have $24 plus tax in your account.

That day in 1991 changed my life. What is your magic harmonica moment? Are you ready to embrace the moment, and choose to focus on your passion? The opportunities are always there. Sometimes it just takes a magic harmonica to show you the way.

Chapter 3

Fun Is a Choice, Passion Is a Choice, Happiness Is a Choice

Life does not cease to be funny when people die any more than it ceases to be serious when people laugh.

—George Bernard Shaw

The large crowd waited patiently for the ballroom doors to open. The finale of the *William Tell* Overture signaled the start to find the perfect seat. As trumpets blared, 400 smiling employees of a large insurance company stampeded to their chairs. In less than two minutes, they were seated and ready for hotel chicken, steak, or stuffed red pepper.[1]

The room buzzed. Employees and executives mingled, smiled, and connected. Something awesome was about to happen. One of their leaders, a vice president and actuary, walked on stage wearing a very tight pseudo–Lone Ranger outfit. He called it "robin's eggshell blue." He had a mask. He had lots of fringes. The crowd ate it up. As he gave out awards and recognized various individuals, he punctuated everything by drawing his toy gun. He had perfect timing, and the crowd loved it.

For a little more than two hours and the price of a hotel chicken lunch, employees celebrated, received applause and recognition for a great year, relaxed, and had fun. And when lunch finished, the employees returned to work, most with a bounce in their step.

It is a simple formula. Break from work + free lunch + actuary dressed as the Lone Ranger + recognition = fun. Why cannot more companies figure this out? Fun wins again. Fun should always win. Now, more than ever, we need to instigate, encourage, and demand fun. Sometimes, we even must fight for it. We are all working harder and longer. Take your pick of recent frustrations: the economy, a recent merger or layoff, global events, reduced benefits, or any daily corporate change.

Fun is our secret weapon. Fun will always win against the stress, frustration, and impatience of change and uncertainty. Fun will increase passion, productivity, and loyalty. Fun energizes our passion for the day-to-day work. It is our fuel, and for many companies it is in short supply.

I think we are afraid to have fun. We are afraid the fun will interrupt our business. We might offend someone. We do not have time for fun. We are not a fun company. Do any of these myths sound familiar? Companies are allowing these myths to dictate meeting agendas and suck the energy from every office, job site, and conference room. Have you ever attended a conference devoid of fun? Meeting zombies walk through convention centers, wearing enormous name tags and clutching free polyester bags.[2] At around noon, give them chicken and a strange rice pilaf, and they will continue in their zombie state for another four to five hours.

My experience is that everyone craves fun. Laughter creates an energy and spirit within the room, building momentum. A fun meeting is a meeting remembered. Audience members are more open to the business messages. More importantly, they retain and apply the business messages. An audience having fun is engaged in the communication of the meeting. Successful meetings get audiences involved and participating.

My first job, I worked at a movie theater. I cleaned the popcorn machine. I picked up other people's trash. I wore a red vest. When

I came home from work, I smelled like hot dogs and butter. I made $2.85 an hour.[3] It was one of the best jobs I ever had.

When you are 15 and working at a movie theater, it is easy to make the choice to have fun. I came to work every day and made it fun. Sure, at times I thought my manager was an evil dictator who had one mission: figure out new ways to clean the movie theater. We would wash walls. We would polish the brass. We removed gum from the carpet. And yes, I worked on holidays. One winter, I worked New Year's Eve during a blizzard.

I had to suffer through projects that I thought were beneath my skill level as a trained concessionaire at a suburban movie theater. One summer, I was Cowboy Bob. You see, during the summer, the movie theater had special showings for kids. Each week, twice a day, hundreds of kids would swarm into the movie theater in a feeding frenzy for *Chitty Chitty Bang Bang*. Parents would drop off their children at the theater with a couple of bucks stuffed in their pockets for candy. The kids would watch the movie, cause mayhem and havoc, and run around like a rampaging herd of buffalo on a sugar high. During that apocalyptic summer, I had to wear an Old West hat, vest, and badge and be Cowboy Bob. Cowboy Bob's primary job was to keep the peace during *Chitty Chitty Bang Bang*. Cowboy Bob solved problems. Looking for your seat? Ask Cowboy Bob. Some kids are kicking your seat? Get Cowboy Bob. Popcorn spilled? Find Cowboy Bob.

If I ever work as an international spy and am subjected to torture, I have full confidence that nothing in my enemy's arsenal could match the summer I spent as Cowboy Bob with several hundred screaming children hopped up on a cocktail of soda, popcorn, and Hot Tamales, repeatedly watching *Chitty Chitty Bang Bang*.

No matter the circumstances, my friends and I figured out a way to have fun. There are no other options when you are 15. If I am going to clean popcorn machines, walk around a movie theater dressed

Fun Is a Choice, Passion Is a Choice, Happiness Is a Choice

as Cowboy Bob, and watch *Chitty Chitty Bang Bang* for $2.85 an hour, I am damn well going to have fun.

It is a pretty easy choice to have fun when we are kids. Unfortunately, when we become adults, we start letting other people make the choice for us. We allow other people to determine our energy, passion, and fun. We let our colleagues and customers, friends, managers, partners, and vendors decide our happiness. When we do that, we are never very happy or passionate. We have given up ownership and responsibility.

Why Would You Choose Anything Other than Fun?

Fun is our fuel for creativity, leadership, passion, and success. Yet we do not really spend any time thinking about fun. Anybody can have fun. We just have to make the choice.

One of the reasons we do not have fun is that we have low expectations of ourselves. Many of my clients caution me before I speak to their group of bankers/lawyers/doctors/engineers/accountants/IT managers that they are boring/shy/introverted/dull and that it will be very difficult for me to get them to come out of their shell/engage in the activities/laugh and have fun. Accountants are boring, they tell me. Doctors are very serious, they say. Lawyers do not laugh, I am reminded. For that matter, any job that does not involve private jets, free food, $30,000 gift baskets, and a personal trainer/chef/butler/maid/concierge is not supposed to be fun.

Guess what? It usually takes about 10 seconds before I have the bankers/lawyers/doctors/engineers/accountants/IT managers laughing. Everyone is creative. Everyone has the ability to have fun. I just have different expectations for my audience. After more than 2,500 presentations for just about every industry, I know everyone wants to laugh and have fun. Everyone has creative ability. It is about creating the opportunity and a positive environment, which I will discuss in other chapters. It is also about making a choice.

Improvisation is about choices. When I invite volunteers on stage to participate in an improvisation game, they choose to have fun. Some are more successful than others, but everyone has fun. Sure, part of their attitude is due to the opportunity and positive support, but part of it is also about choice. Why do they choose to have fun? Is it because the game is not serious? We can have fun no matter our industry or job. In fact, we must have fun. Without fun, there is no passion. Without passion, where is our energy and success?

If you do not believe me, visit a high school or college and watch a group of teenagers. When I speak to students, their energy and creativity amaze me. They run to the stage to volunteer for the exercises. They throw themselves into every activity with energy and passion. These same kids will become bankers, lawyers, doctors, engineers, accountants, and IT managers. What happens to them? Where does the energy go? It cannot all be because of a sugar rush.

It is about choices. We slowly start making choices that zap our energy and happiness. We take a job for the wrong reasons. We choose our career based on earning potential and not happiness potential. We make decisions based on what other people think instead of what we want. Soon, we are working without passion. Our creative fuel tank is emptier than a Friday night sitcom.

We have to take responsibility for our choices. When I work with smaller groups, I play a game where the participants have to create a commercial or advertising jingle for a product that does not exist. They work in teams of five to eight people and have less than 10 minutes to develop their commercial and define their product's features and benefits. The short time frame forces them to make the right choices to achieve success as a team. Each group is full of energy as they develop their commercial or jingle. They are having fun. After each

Fun Is a Choice, Passion Is a Choice, Happiness Is a Choice

group performs, I ask them about their process. The answers are always the same:

- Because of the time restraint, the group was focused.

- The group was very open to each other's ideas.

- Everyone participated.

- When they received positive support from each other, they wanted to give more ideas.

- Everyone had a positive attitude during the exercise.

- Everyone had fun.

- The energy created during the exercise made it easier to work together and meet the objectives.

- Their ideas created more ideas.

Even though the objective of this exercise had nothing to do with their jobs, I wanted to prove a point. The group made the choice to have fun during the exercise. By choosing to have fun and by enjoying the process, their attitude changed and forced them to make the right choice in how they worked and communicated with their team. The result is a successful and creative team.[4]

To prove my point further, I ask the same groups to choose a serious challenge they each face at their jobs. I ask them to develop ideas or create a plan to successfully meet the challenge. Again, I give them a short time frame to come up with their ideas. Immediately, the room becomes very quiet as the groups start working on their very serious ideas. I stop the process and remind the groups what made them successful in the last exercise. Just because our topic is more serious, we still need to use the energy and attitude that made us successful during the first part of the exercise.

If I give the group a "serious" objective, they immediately make the choice to reduce their energy. They choose to eliminate the fun. After I point this out to the group, their attitude starts to change. Seconds later, the energy rises in the room. Participants are enjoying the process again. They are still focused on their "serious" challenge, but now they have made a choice about their attitude. The energy increases. The laughter increases. The creativity increases.

No matter the situation, we must take control of our choices. We all face tough circumstances that are outside of our control. The one thing that is always under our control is our attitude. We come up with too many reasons not to have fun. Here are four of the common myths about fun.

Myth #1: We Are Afraid the Fun Will Interrupt Our Business

Yes, fun will interrupt the business. That is the whole point. Your mind needs to take mental breaks, even for a few seconds, throughout the day. One dose of laughter, and the mind becomes more aware and focused. You rarely see people laugh hysterically one moment and then fall asleep the next. I am sure there is a scientist right now somewhere in New Mexico proving that mice rarely fall asleep after laughing. You can look it up.

Fun does not have to interrupt. Fun does not take the place of something else. In another chapter, I talk about the sprinkles on the cupcake. Fun is the sprinkles on the cupcake. Fun can be part of business. Remember your favorite high school teacher? He or she made learning fun. Adults are no different than high school kids learning American history. Adults just have less acne.

Try something different. There are thousands of ideas to deliver important messages in a fun and entertaining way. You only must create the opportunity.

Fun Is a Choice, Passion Is a Choice, Happiness Is a Choice

Myth #2: We Might Offend Someone

Fun comes in many forms. Do your research and understand your group. What is fun for one person might not be very fun for others in the group. There will always be somebody not having fun. The problem is when you allow the person who will never have fun—no matter what you do—to make decisions for the entire group. It is best to ignore the grumpy, bitter guy in the puffer vest.

Fun should not offend or make people feel uncomfortable. Fun should not be at the expense of others. Be creative. If you need outside help, hire professionals and check references.

Sometimes people need a little nudge into fun. I have seen dozens of scavenger hunts start the same way. People mill about. People whine. People act too cool for a scavenger hunt. And then suddenly, everyone starts to participate in the scavenger hunt. People who were too cool for school become the most competitive. People have fun. It happens every time.

Myth #3: We Do Not Have Time for Fun

Fun does not take much time. There are plenty of ways to have fun with little time. At a recent client's meeting, *[IDEA ALERT]* attendees kept asking me, "Do you have the gold coin?" I had no idea what they were talking about. Later, I realized employees were passing around a Sacagawea dollar coin. If someone asked you for the coin and you had the coin, you had to give up the coin. At the end of the day, whoever had the coin won a gift certificate. This activity took zero time from the day's presentations yet created fun interactions between employees and generated energy and excitement. This was also the first time I have written the name *Sacagawea*.

Fun can be simple. Fun can be achieved with little effort. Do your research. Be creative. Ask the event team or other employees to list fun activities they have seen at other meetings or jobs. Here is

20

Make the Right Choice

another tip: ask your team for ideas from children's birthday parties. With a few adjustments, just about every game played by children can be used at a work gathering.

Myth #4: We Are Not a Fun Company

Almost every client tells me they are not fun. They tell me their people do not participate. Their employees are very serious. As my mother-in-law says, "That information is about as useless as owl crap on a hickory branch."

If you really believe this and you do not try, you will not have fun. It is amazing how many meeting planners have said to me, "This is the first time we have incorporated humor and fun into our meeting." And I look at them as if they had just swallowed a small compact car.

We all want to have fun. We all want to laugh. I do not think most people wake up in the morning with a goal of not having fun. It is our job to find the right ingredients that will create fun for the group.

The two most important ingredients are opportunity and a positive environment. When was the last time you created a fun opportunity at a meeting? It is up to you to create that opportunity.

Some ideas will not work. Some will work. Stay in the game. Keep trying to find ways to add fun to your work culture.

Fun is also simple. It really does not take much time, budget, or energy. It just takes willingness. Here are seven ideas for managers to promote, encourage, and instigate fun:

1. **Create surprise and silliness.** The Lone Ranger vice president is the perfect example. I have seen executives dress up as a Roman emperor, cowboy, Greek Olympian, super hero, and everything else. It always works. Work is serious. Business is serious. It is okay to lighten up a little with a touch of silliness.

Fun Is a Choice, Passion Is a Choice, Happiness Is a Choice

Here is another example: One of my best friends works at a telecommunications company. They had a large chess piece (about four feet high) in their office. It would appear in someone's office one day and reappear the next day somewhere else. Sometimes they would take the chess piece to meetings with them. It was silly. Sometimes it was given as an award. If you were having a rough day, it was guaranteed the chess piece would show up in your office. The recipient would always smile.

I remember when my friend (who was in the Army Reserve) was called up and sent to Kuwait. One day, his colleagues mailed him the chess piece. My friend carried this four-foot chess piece around the base and took pictures: in the mess hall, on a tank, in the latrine. Everyone on base laughed at my friend's chess piece during the impromptu photo session. They offered photo ideas. He sent the photos back to his friends. His friends at work loved the photos. One four-foot chess piece created fun on two continents, one war zone, and one large corporation.

What is your four-foot chess piece? Fun sometimes comes from unlikely places. The common ingredient is always a little silliness mixed with a little surprise and some imagination.

2. **Create recognition and celebration.** A little positive support and recognition is a huge ingredient to fun. Be creative and different. Telling someone "Thank you" or "I appreciate you" is the greatest gift you can ever give. And it does not take any money, planning, budget, or a PowerPoint presentation with an upside-down triangle.

- Create a "thank you" bulletin board in the break room.
- Give out a funny trophy each week.

- Take someone out to lunch.

- When I host award programs, I always suggest the client create a slide show to play during dinner with photos and work/personal achievements of everyone in the room. Ask employees and managers to submit their achievements. You might only be giving out 12 awards, but you just recognized everyone in the room with the slide show.

There are hundreds, if not thousands, of ways to celebrate and recognize employees for their work, dedication, and excellence. And every way you find will foster, encourage, and create fun.[5]

3. **Energize meetings.** Skit night is a big deal. What is skit night? "You can't miss skit night," I was told repeatedly. "What time are you coming to skit night?" I was asked. Believe me, I am not missing skit night.

Skit night is the highlight of the annual leadership meeting for one of my large apartment management clients. On the opening night, the CEO and COO give a presentation. And then skit night happens. Several of the regions are tasked with performing a skit that can and does include everything from acting, video, music, lip syncs, and "dancing." Each region performs every other year to increase the anticipation.

Each skit was about their culture, current trends, executives, state of the business, or just about everything else. Between the videos and the stage performance, dozens of people were involved in each performance.

When I saw skit night, I was amazed, delighted, and entertained. I spoke to the CEO after the meeting. He could not have been happier. You see, skit night has nothing to do with the performance. Sure, it adds some fun, energy, and laughter

Fun Is a Choice, Passion Is a Choice, Happiness Is a Choice

to the annual meeting. Skit night is about the time spent back at the office planning, writing, producing, and rehearsing skit night. Managers and employees from each department spend time together creating their skit. Everyone in the region is involved at some point.

Skit night is a release. Everyone working on the common objective of skit night is an equal. Different departments working together on skit night builds camaraderie, respect, loyalty, passion, and friendship. Those are the same skills that will be needed during a crisis. Skit night is fun. And just one more reason why the company with the annual tradition of skit night is consistently named one of the best places to work in the country.

4. **Promote innovation.** I was recently invited to speak at a medical technology company's Innovation Week. Each day offered a different session that lasted one to two hours. The sessions ranged from a panel sharing innovation achievements from the past year to participating in a brainstorming session for new ideas. Different speakers were brought in to discuss and build innovation skills.

All the sessions occurred on site and were attended on a voluntary basis. Employees and managers were encouraged to attend with door prizes and giveaways.

The sessions were fun and were built around an important skill that builds success. Fun can also be about business. Taking a few hours once a year to promote and encourage innovation offers year-round dividends. Most of the sessions were focused on serious topics and creating ideas to help build their business, which means saving lives and helping their patients that use their devices.

The innovation program was about their business, but also a break from their routine. It was special and different. Again, these are the ingredients for fun.

5. **Donate your time.** Donating time as a team creates a fun, rewarding experience. I have participated in dozens of programs over the years. And I have yet to hear someone complain. There are hundreds of possibilities and opportunities to create fun and give back to the community. Here are three of my favorites:

   A. *Team shopping excursion.* Choose a worthy recipient organization. Split the group into small teams of six or less. Give them a mall gift certificate, a shopping list, and a one-hour time frame. Stand back and let the shopping begin. My group ran from store to store with our list, looking for the best discounts. We wanted to see how much we could buy on our list. Every group did the same thing, running through the mall with energy and excitement. The best part was when the organization came to the meeting to accept the donation.

   B. *Creative United Way fundraisers.* Many companies run United Way campaigns through paycheck donations. The annual United Way campaign (or any charity) is a perfect opportunity for fun and creativity. One client had a talent show. Another client made a miniature golf course at the office. Any visitor (vendors, partners, customers, delivery people) would pay a few dollars to play the course. One client had a cubicle decoration contest. Contact your local United Way, and they can probably give you 100 great ideas.

   C. *Spend a day giving back.* Many of my clients have given their most precious gift: time. Spending a day (or even a few hours) cleaning, painting, building, reading, or helping brings people together. It is not just fun for the employees. It is rewarding.

D. *Technology awareness day.* My railroad client sponsors a technology awareness day for area high school juniors and seniors to encourage careers in technology. The program is on a Saturday at their corporate campus and is completely staffed and volunteered by employees. It was obvious the program was as rewarding to the employees as it was to the students.

6. **Improve your surroundings.** I recently visited a client in their office. When I walked in, I noticed a huge painting, separated into small vibrant squares. I mentioned the painting to my client. Her department created the painting over the course of several days. Each team member chose one of the squares for their portion of the painting. Four people could work on the painting at one time. Each box within the painting represented the team member's style, interests, and personality.

Their first objective was to enhance their surroundings. The training department moved into a new office with blank, white walls, which they were told not to paint. The second objective was a fun activity that brought the team together. The third objective was to highlight the team's individuality and personality. For the price of some paint and a large canvas, the department created an easy and fun activity.

Every day they walk in the office they see the result and are reminded of the teamwork, passion, creativity, and inspiration that went into the painting. When someone new walks into the department, usually their first comment is about the painting. Employees show off "their" square and talk about the art. Like all great art masterpieces hanging in museums, it brings people together. Except this one only cost a few dollars.

7. **Compete.** Competition is always fun. I always laugh when a corporate scavenger hunt (or similar competitive activity) begins. There is always a group that is too cool. They hang back, crack jokes, and resist. And then a funny thing happens. They see everyone having fun. Or they cannot resist the urge to help their friends. Or they cannot resist their urge to do something. Whatever it is, a transformation happens. The "too cool for school" kids participate and have fun. Grumpiness erupts into giddiness.

No matter the company. No matter the industry. A scavenger hunt or a silly build-a-rocket-out-of-aluminum-foil-and-toothpicks activity is always going to be more fun than another day of processing, accounting, selling, distributing, or insert-job-activity here. My favorite competitions are the ones that are about being "best" at their given job. A quick-service restaurant client has competitions for the best car hops. The best are invited to the annual meeting to compete. An apartment association client sponsors a skills competition for employees in maintenance. I loved watching each company cheer on their colleagues. I do not think I have ever been in a louder, more fun environment at a meeting.

Fun is different for everyone. Still, there are some common ingredients that create fun. Fun does not have to cost anything or take a lot of time. And in the corporate world right now, the fun bar is so low that it really does not take much to hit a home run.

Find your fun. Encourage it. Fight for it. Find your Lone Ranger or four-foot chess piece. Give back. What is your skit night? What is your Innovation Week? More importantly, what is your fun?

Fun Is a Choice, Passion Is a Choice, Happiness Is a Choice

Quick Ideas

Your goal every day is to go home happy, energized, and passionate. It is your choice. When we give that choice to our managers, customers, coworkers, vendors, the stock market, the government, and others, we are not very happy. Take it back. Who are you allowing to determine your happiness through their words and actions? For example, a driver cuts you off on the highway. You scream and yell. You are angry. Your blood pressure rises. You just let a complete stranger control your emotions. Someone you do not even know is affecting your blood pressure and your health. Will you remember him cutting you off in traffic for the rest of your life? No.

Take the choice back. Get greedy. Take the choice back from everyone. You should have ownership of your happiness because you are the only person who really knows what makes you happy. When you take back the ownership of your attitude, you will wake up a happier, more passionate, and more energized person because it is now truly your choice.

Chapter 4

Make the Right Choice: Six Sprinkles on the Leadership Cupcake

A leader is best when people barely know he exists, when his work is done, his aim fulfilled, they will say: we did it ourselves.

—Lao Tzu

Here is my full disclosure: I love a manager who can strut into a room wearing a crazy costume. A recent client made her way into the manager's conference as a mermaid. I think there was even a fishing pole attached. The audience loved it. I am not sure if all the world's problems could be solved if our leaders were required to appear as a mermaid or other mythical creature. I am betting we could knock out one or two. Somehow, I just have more respect for someone when they present information dressed as a mermaid.[1]

As you read this, there are two possible reactions: "Yeah, I once dressed as a Roman general/race car driver/disco dancer/pick your favorite decade outfit/Austin Powers/*Saturday Night Live* character to open a conference/inspire the team/give out awards/wish someone a happy birthday, and it was awesome/electric/inspiring/hilarious."

Or your reaction could be: "I don't do costumes."

If your reaction is the latter, you probably are not going to like my six observations of great leadership. I admit that costumes are silly. To me, a little silly can inspire respect, passion, and success. The world could use a little silly. And my guess is that your office could use a little silly.

Leadership books are like finding a penny on the ground. They are everywhere, and most of us have stopped picking them up and instead just keep walking.[2] Sure, business books cover all the elements of great, serious leadership. What about some of the things the books do not cover? What about the sprinkles on the cupcake? One of my favorite clients (and a regional vice president of a large company) always told me you cannot forget about the sprinkles on the cupcake. The sprinkles are the little extra that make everything better.

Maybe it is time to pick up the penny again, but look at it differently. I have worked with around 2,500 different groups. Luckily, I have the chance to meet hundreds (maybe thousands)[3] of corporate presidents, vice presidents, CEOs, and every kind of manager. I observe and watch. Through the years, I have seen good and not so good leaders.

Recently, a group of managers decided to read this book and discuss each chapter in a leadership book club. They asked whether I could call in and discuss leadership and the book. I was honored and a little surprised they had chosen my little book. I called in, and we had a wonderful conversation. Through our discussion, I was asked, "What makes a great leader?"

Here are my six observations that allow leaders to be successful. They are my sprinkles on the cupcake. Dressing as a mermaid is optional.

1. **Engage and participate.** I encounter all kinds of managers when I speak to various groups and organizations. I was asked to speak to a small group of managers. The person giving my introduction had not even finished before the company president walked out the door. The person giving my introduction, part of the leadership team, also did not stay for my presentation. What do you think this says to the group of managers?

A. "I know everything, so there is no reason to listen to the person I hired to speak to you."

B. "I am better than everyone else in the room."

C. "My time is more valuable."

D. "I do not interact with the 'lower' managers."

E. "I want to be first in line for the deli lunch boxes."

These thoughts may or may not be true. I have no doubt everyone in the room thought at least one of them. There is nothing that frustrates me more than a leader that does not participate. If you expect your team to experience it, then you, as their leader, should also participate. Engage with your team.

Participate in every activity, even the ones that are silly. You might learn something. You will also gain valuable respect from your team. I think great leaders stand beside their team when they lead. They are part of the team, not separate from the team. You will always lose more by not participating.

At a recent conference, I had three managers playing a teamwork and communication game. They were playing an improv game that is a variation of "Telephone" plus some charades, plus some other improv elements. All three had to act out a roller coaster (location), ballerina (occupation), and a porcupine (object). The three volunteers leave the room where they can't hear anything. The audience shouts out the three suggestions. The first manager comes back in, joins me on stage, and I communicate the three messages (only speaking a made-up language called Gibberish). Then the second manager comes into the room. The first manager then communicates the three messages (hopefully she has the correct answers). Finally, the second manager communicates to the third manager (who has just entered the room).

Make the Right Choice: Six Sprinkles on the Leadership Cupcake

The goal is to get the last person at the end of the telephone string to correctly guess the location, occupation, and object.

The second manager was twirling around like a ballerina to the third manager. The third manager refused to be a ballerina. I asked. The audience even cheered and applauded, hoping to boost his confidence. Nope. He refused. I did not want to force or press him. We just all moved on to the next portion of the game.

Guess how many attendees mentioned his reaction to me at dinner? More than you think. The worst decision he made was to not engage and participate in the game. He could have just twirled around. Nobody asked him to do Swan Lake. He just had to try. I am sure he thought he would look silly and it would be embarrassing.

He chose not to engage. What do you think the other managers thought of him? He just did the worst thing you can do on stage. He quit on his team. You can do anything you want on stage. You just cannot quit.

2. **Admit mistakes.** During my discussion with the book club, one of the leaders mentioned she had two small teams. She invited one team (five people) for a discussion followed by lunch. She did not invite the other team (two people). Each team does separate jobs, so she thought the small team would not be interested. She asked my opinion.

To me, great leadership is about inclusiveness and finding common ground. Great leaders bring people together and find commonalities. We can always learn from each other. I think she should have at least given the small team the option to attend. Let us not forget there was a free lunch involved.

As we talked through everything, the manager realized she had made a mistake. Her plan was to admit her mistake and plan more opportunities for the two teams to interact and learn from each other.

Yes, it is hard to admit our mistakes. We all make them. The great leaders admit their mistakes and find a way to correct them.

3. **Ask questions.** We all want opportunity in our jobs. And opportunity is different for all of us. We could want more responsibility, customer interaction, travel, training, or the opportunity to present ideas. Some of us are very good about raising our hands and asking for opportunity. Some are not. As leaders, we must ask our team what opportunity they need to be happy. You will be surprised by the answer, because it is not more money. That happiness only lasts until the next paycheck, and then we are right back at the beginning, looking for something else.

You will also be surprised by how easy it is to give that opportunity to your team member. The best part is the employee becomes more energized and passionate. The result of that passion is always success. Ask your team one question: What opportunity do you need to be happy? And then ask the question: What can I do to make the people around me more successful? Find the answers and act on them.

4. **Avoid trying to make everyone happy.** Sometimes a new client will explain they have a few malcontents in their company. They never like anything new. They are cynical. They have a bad attitude. I have heard it all. They then ask me, "What am I going to do to engage the malcontents?" I have a simple plan: I couldn't care less. They are not my problem. They are your problem because you hired them. Companies

and leaders spend too much time, money, and effort trying to make everyone happy. It is not going to happen. Think of the classic bell curve. There are three groups:

A. The beginning of the curve. These people are your stars. If you walked in and said we were eating only carrots for lunch this week, they would clap their hands, jump up, and shout, "Carrots! I love carrots!"

B. The middle part of the curve. This is the big part of the curve or bell. These employees can go either way. They like carrots. Sometimes they think about carrots. You must convince them that carrots are good for them. They also want leadership. Motivate these team members. Inspire them to succeed. And they will love those carrots.

C. The end of the curve is where the malcontents live. These are the "bye-bye" people. You'll learn more about them in a later chapter. They don't care about goals or making the customer (internal or external) happy. They don't care about mission statements, teamwork, customer service, or anything else. Mentally, they are gone. They are "bye-bye." They are not happy. And nothing is really going to make them happy. And they certainly don't want any of your damn carrots.

Spend your time rewarding and appreciating the stars and motivating and inspiring the team in the bell curve. Try to engage the "bye-bye" people. You must at least give them a chance, and you have done your due diligence. In another chapter, I discuss creating opportunity and positive support. Yes, even the "bye-bye" people want opportunity and positive support. Hopefully, they will participate and help the team create success. If they do not make the choice, then it might be time for them to find opportunity and happiness at another company.

5. **Communicate.** During the leadership book club, one of the managers mentioned that there was a huge change in her team. A key leader was leaving. Her team was worried because of impending change. What should she do?

We discussed three steps:

A. Always communicate what is happening. If you don't fill the space with news, they will fill it with rumor. And the rumor and conjecture they create will always be negative. That is just how it works. Communicate what is happening and the next steps in the process of finding a new manager. Fill the void with positive and correct information.

B. During the transition, make sure you communicate your appreciation and support for their hard work and passion. Positive support is a gift. And it doesn't take a budget. It just takes a few seconds.

C. Reward the employees who have taken on more work and filled the gaps during the transition. Surprise them with a coffee run. Give everyone a birthday card on the same day (even if it is not their birthday). Take the team to lunch. Just tell them how much you appreciate them.

6. **Laugh and have fun.** Yep, we have circled back to dressing up as a mermaid. It is up to you to wear or not wear a silly costume. Just open up a little more. Be a part of the fun and games. Find ways to laugh with your team. Laughter is our great common denominator. It humanizes us.

Every time I bring the "big boss" on stage to participate in an exercise with me, the audience goes wild. They love it. After the presentation, everyone talks about the "big boss" participating and having fun. It is amazing the respect and admiration they gain by stepping out of their comfort zone.

Make the Right Choice: Six Sprinkles on the Leadership Cupcake

There is nothing that bonds and connects people like laughter. If you show me a leader with humility and that can laugh at themselves, I know they are respected and admired.

Those are my six sprinkles on the leadership cupcake. I hope they help you become a better leader and avoid some of the pitfalls. I always fall back on my favorite message: you must stay in the game. Look up any great leader in history. Their story is sure to be filled with challenges, mistakes, and obstacles. The difference is that the great leaders didn't quit. They stayed in the game. They learned something new. They worked harder. They got out of their comfort zone. And some of them even dressed up like mermaids.

Chapter 5

Beware of the Dumb Ass Manager (D.A.M.): Observations on Leadership

A sense of humor is part of the art of leadership, of getting along with people, of getting things done.

—Dwight D. Eisenhower

I have worked with many awesome leaders and managers over the years. I have also worked with a few not so awesome leaders. I watch and study how they play the improvisation games, interact with team members, and how they approach the situation. Very quickly, I noticed patterns and correlations between their actions and participation in the exercises and their leadership style.

My observations are not scientific. They are not based on extensive research, interviews, or analysis. They are simply based on paying attention to what is happening in the moment. Here are a few numbers: I have presented at more than 2,500 events, with an average of 12 audience volunteers per keynote. More than 30,000 people have jumped on stage with me. I observe and watch how each person plays the game. I use these observations in how I communicate to my clients, to the executive participants who join me on stage, and to the audience. Body language, tone of voice, eye movement, speech patterns, even the speed of their walk from their seat to the stage helps me evaluate their attitude and ability to play the improvisation game.

I often tell my clients that you can tell quite a bit about a person by how they play improvisation games—or any games. I can tell who is creative, who is a follower, who is a leader, who is a micromanager, who is a good listener, who is a bad listener, and who does and does not deal well with change. And those are just a few of the habits, personalities, and attitudes I observe. By observing their characteristics and traits, I can better understand how they will react during the performance. I also want to give them the best chance for success by placing them in the right role. If I read someone as tentative, I might place them in a role in the game that is easier. For the more demanding roles, I will place the more extroverted audience volunteer in that spot.

When someone plays a game, they revert to their natural instincts and characteristics. Try an experiment one evening with your friends. Play a new board game, and watch how each person interacts. Does one person take control as the leader and explain the instructions? Is there a person who is very helpful to the other players in explaining strategy? Is there a person who is quick to applaud and give verbal support? How about a person who gets angry when the game is not going his or her way?

See what I mean? In the very unlikely circumstance that I find myself running a company, I would play improvisation games during the hiring process. I would sit behind a two-way mirror with a cheese and fruit platter and watch potential employees. Do you think companies would buy this idea from me? Can I trademark this? Seriously, whom do I speak to about this idea?

We can all spot a great manager. They support the team, create opportunity and positive support, and build a foundation for success. A great leader helps the people around them be successful. An awesome manager cares about their people and gives them room to take ownership and grow.

This chapter is about identifying the bad managers who infect every industry. I remember a manager early in my career, a cigarette dangling from her mouth, yelling and cussing at me to work faster on a deadline. That is not even my favorite bad manager story. If I am in a circle of people, trying to one up each other in stories, I always pull out the tale of a bad manager, balloons, and potpourri.[1] When I was in public relations, I had a manager who mailed huge bags of potpourri, tied with a balloon, to potential clients to win business. He spent hours on this project, and he roped in a marketing assistant to help. I can still see that assistant struggling to box up the balloons and potpourri. I am not joking. If this sounds like a scene from the television show *The Office*, you are correct. When Michael Scott tries to land new business with gift baskets, I was rolling on the floor because it hit so close to home.

What do you do if you encounter one of these managers? My simple answer is to start looking for a new opportunity. Some of these bad managers will cause you too much stress and extra work. Your happiness and passion are what is important. Find a manager and opportunity that will celebrate you, encourage you, fulfill you, and increase your passion.

Okay, here are just a few of my observations of bad managers in the wild.

The D.A.M.

The Dumb Ass Manager (D.A.M.) does not listen. They may look as if they are listening, but whatever you are telling them is traveling through their ears into a time-space continuum where the information is trapped. This is why the manager does not do well in the improvisation games. The manager is not very supportive or helpful to the other teammates in achieving the game's objective. Usually, the D.A.M. is overly concerned with how the audience perceives them. Sometimes, they will sabotage the game, thinking their efforts are funny and are perceived as cool and in control. The opposite is true. The D.A.M. is perceived as half-assing their roles.

By worrying about perceptions and attitudes beyond their control, the D.A.M. is not in the moment of the game. To be successful

Beware of the Dumb Ass Manager (D.A.M.)

in improvisation games, you have to work and communicate in the moment. You cannot think about the last game, the next game, your issues, what people think, or anything other than the game.

This manager has communication issues:

1. Try to communicate an issue to this manager. It will be ignored or misunderstood. "I thought you meant this," rolls off their tongue as easy as water lapping up on a beach.

2. "I did email/text that to you." Guess what? They did not. This is another common phrase. The best part is you will have receipts.

3. "I told . . ." and then add the vendor/partner/colleague/customer and then add information/instructions/or requests. Would you believe the part after "I told . . ." never happens?

The D.A.M. only likes their ideas. They become obsessed with a trivial idea that creates more work for everyone yet does not add value or results. The D.A.M blames more than supports. The D.A.M. micromanages their team so much that the team will revolt.

My wife worked with a hurricane D.A.M. that combined six terrible traits: micromanager, disorganized and not focused on details, blamed instead of supported, refused to delegate, took on work that should have been delegated and then was left undone, and was a poor communicator that said one thing and did another.

One of these traits is a D.A.M. All these traits combined creates a mutant D.A.M. that terrorizes the countryside like Godzilla, causing stress, loss of passion, anger, and resentment.

The Micromanager

A micromanager will crush your soul. They smash your passion as if they were stomping grapes.

The micromanager wants you to do the project like they would do the project. A friend did social media for an organization. The manager would constantly correct their work, change their work, tell them what to do and how they should do the work, and then sometimes just do it themselves. As I wrote this paragraph, a little bile burped up into my mouth. A few weeks of this went by, and my friend, fed up, did what Johnny Paycheck sings about in probably the greatest work song ever, "Take This Job and Shove It."

Why continue doing the job when someone is constantly micromanaging you? Here is a quick story about a manager that did not micromanage.

After a recent event, produced by a volunteer organization, the board and team gathered for a festive party. The awesome president took time and said a few words about each board member and how they made the event a success. The moment inspired me. One of the board members then told the awesome president how much they appreciated his trust, faith, and support. She mentioned how he supported them in their jobs. He did not micromanage, she said. He trusted each member to do their job. It was truly an awesome moment. What did he receive in return? A passionate, energized team that produced a successful event.

The Terrible Communicator

Look up toward the night sky and count the stars, and you will still not reach the number of ways a manager can poorly communicate. Here are a few of my favorites:

1. The "never say anything" manager. I once had a manager who stopped talking to me. I reported to him, and he stopped talking to me. So I started reporting to one of the agency heads.

2. The "that is not what I said" manager. This manager thinks they communicated. Something goes wrong. And then the manager tries to cover. I do not know if they live in an alter-

nate reality or believe they didn't say what they said even though everyone has the emails or texts that say otherwise.

3. The "I am just going to keep talking and use different words but not really say anything" manager. Lord, help us.

The Blame Everyone Else Manager

This manager loves to blame anyone close. The best part is when they blame someone for their mistake, and that same person kept receipts and shows the email chain.

The Martyr

This manager is related to the "blame everyone else" manager. They want everyone to feel pity. People are nice, so they say this person "means well" or "has a good heart." And then the manager sucks the soul out of the team, and you realize "meaning well" and "having a good heart" are overrated.

The Disorganized Manager

This manager forgets *everything*. Do they take notes? Do they make lists? Do they have spreadsheets? I have no idea because they do not remember what was said, what was agreed upon, or the plan. Would it make it better if I told you they "have a good heart," "mean well," and "are a really nice person"?

The "I Will Take Care of That" and Refuses to Delegate Manager

This manager wants to do everything themselves. They trust nobody. They constantly say, "I will take care of that." And the work never gets done. A great leader delegates the work to the team, trusts them, and creates the foundation for their success.

The Bully Manager

This manager digs in and tries to bully everyone into agreeing with them. They obsess on one idea or thought and will bully everyone to their side. They hammer you. They will not budge. Sometimes they want you to think they are budging. There is no budge. There is no plan for a budge. Sometimes they just keep talking, using different words that all end up to be: "Do what I want you to do."

The Aloha Manager

There are two distinct variations of the aloha manager (A.M.):

1. The *aloha alpha* version is attempting to connect with their employees by showing a willingness to dress in a "fun" outfit. More than likely, the A.M. wears their trusty Hawaiian shirt for retreats, conferences, employee picnics, and other large employee gatherings. They are harmless and usually want the team to succeed. They are at least making some kind of effort to have fun.

2. The *aloha beta* version is retired, and the one you really need to guard against. Unfortunately, the aloha manager still very much works for the company and is retired only in their own mind. The A.M. still has the same executive or management duties but mentally is gone. This manager is not interested in growth, change, or management. Be very wary of this manager. The A.M. is still the captain of the boat. They are just not steering the vessel because they are is too busy fishing for marlin off the back. I usually show caution with this manager.

The Bye-Bye Manager

This manager doesn't even stay in the room for the presentation. The B.B.M. expects all the other managers and employees to sit in the room and participate, but they are too busy making phone calls or sending emails. I never could figure out who they were calling or emailing because every employee was currently in the ballroom.

The intensified versions of this manager run around so frantically they end up forgetting anything you told them. They are too busy bouncing from task to task. They are kind of like really fast bumper cars at the state fair. They seem to have purpose, but they are just bumping around without direction.

These managers tend not to communicate very well.

The "Yes, I Would Love to Kiss Your Ass" Manager

Usually, the "yes, I would love to kiss your ass" manager (Y.I.W.L.T.K.Y.A.M.) works directly for a top vice president. The Y.I.W.L.T.K.Y.A.M. does not have the capability to say no to their boss. They can, however, say no to everyone else. The working relationship dynamic between this manager and their boss should be studied by sociologists. The boss is the fraternity/sorority president. The manager is a perpetual fraternity/sorority pledge who will never get into the fraternity/sorority.[2] The manager is very friendly and can keep an eye on the boss from anywhere in the room.

Other strange characteristics include nabbing a seat next to the boss in every situation, dressing like the boss, and being able to produce their manager's PowerPoint presentation on their laptop, flash drive, and/or cell phone within seconds.

It's Not Just About Communication: It Is About Connecting to Your Audience

These are just a few of the managers I have observed over the years. Most managers have a good attitude and want success for the employees and company. Most issues between leadership and employees tend to start with a lack of communication. Actually, it starts with a lack of connection.

A recent client of mine had a manager panel discussion with the employees. For an hour, they answered questions from employees about the direction of the department, upcoming changes, and workload. I watched almost the entire hour of questions and answers. I am pretty sure the managers gave the same answer to every question, or at least that was my impression. I had a hard time following the discussion because the primary words used were "scalability," "optimize," "matrix," "value-add," and "process." I am not really sure if I optimized the process because I couldn't really value-add without the proper scalability.

We really need to stop talking like this. We are not connecting to each other when we use made-up words, empty of true meaning. Speak directly. Speak honestly. Speak clearly.

The employees care about their company and their department. If they didn't, they wouldn't have asked questions and showed concern. I have seen many panel discussions that are awash in apathy. The managers also care; otherwise, they wouldn't have taken the time to have a panel discussion and answer the employee's questions.

What does improvisation teach? The games force the players to make the right decision. Improvisation games don't allow you to disconnect from your teammates. You cannot think about yesterday, the next game, what you have to do that day, your next meeting, or anything else. You have to work in the moment, or the game will fail. As leaders, are we always in the moment when we communicate with our employees? I always tell my audiences, "Ask the volunteers who came on stage what they thought about when they participated in the improvisation games." They can only think about communicating and working together as a team to meet the objective of the game. They are in the moment.

Beware of the Dumb Ass Manager (D.A.M.)

We are at our best when we are in the moment. We are better leaders, communicators, and teammates. We need to spend more time being present and in the moment with our team, customers, and partners.

You must communicate in a supportive, positive manner, or the game fails. More importantly, you have to create an environment where everyone can take initiative. When I invite three volunteers on stage from the audience, I explain the basics of the game. I do not tell them how to play the game, what to say, or what they should do. The participants have the responsibility to take initiative.

Create the Opportunity for Ownership and Initiative

What changes when the participants take initiative? They own the game. It is no longer my game, even though I am starting my fourth decade of performing improvisation professionally and have probably played the game 15,000 times. I could easily tell each of the participants what to say and do during the game. If I did, they certainly would have some measure of success, but they wouldn't have fun. I want them to have a fun, positive attitude. When I don't tell them what to do, they take responsibility and ownership, and their attitude about the experience changes. The result of the ownership is the participants become more creative, have more fun, take more risks, and have a positive, supportive attitude. Isn't that what we want from our managers and employees?

This was a very long chapter. There is a lot to think about. Before moving on to the next chapter, go find a Hawaiian shirt and pretend you are retired for a few hours.

Quick Ideas

The question I am asked the most is, "What do I do about a manager or coworker who is negative and not supportive?" I always answer the same way: "Do you have any duct tape?" After the laughter subsides, I usually say, "Okay, let's be serious. Where can you find duct tape?" There is no perfect answer. All I know is what improvisation has taught me: communication is the best way to find a solution.

- When was the last time you spoke to your manager about what you need to be happy? My advice is to walk into your manager's office and communicate what you need. I am pretty sure it is in your manager's best interest for you to work productively and effectively. Be honest. The manager might not even understand what he or she is doing and how it affects you. Think about what opportunity would reward and fulfill you. Do you want more training? Do you want a different role or responsibility? Communicate what you need to be fulfilled and rewarded at your job. If your manager refuses to provide you the opportunity, then it might be time to look for a different job because you are not going to be happy in your current role.

- As for the coworker whining in the break room, I have the same answer. Does the whining help your creativity? Does the whining help your productivity? Is the negative attitude doing anything positive for you? If not, then politely ask the coworker to leave you out of the bitch sessions. If you continue to say this, your coworkers will realize not to bitch and whine around you. Your office is a society. Years ago, our own society approved of smoking in the workplace. I remember working at a newspaper with people smoking around me. Then our society decided smoking in the workplace was not such a good idea. And we changed.

Whining is the same thing. You can change your society. You just have to stand up and say something. If you were in an elevator and someone lit a cigarette, would you ask them to stop smoking?[3] Well, why don't we ask the person who is whining to stop?

- After a presentation, a woman shared a similar story with me about a few negative coworkers creating a difficult work environment. She had spoken to her manager, but he didn't take any action. She didn't know what to do. I told her there were no easy answers. You have to communicate to your manager and to the employees. What kind of work environment does everyone want? What is going to help everyone find success and happiness? I am pretty sure negative, pissed-off employees will tend to not create a positive and successful work environment.

- It was obvious this woman loved her job. She was passionate about the company. Unfortunately, she was not very happy. She agreed to try communicating her feelings to her manager and to the other employees. She cannot sit passively and wait for some magical change to occur. She has to try and change her environment. Hopefully, she will achieve success. In the end, though, she may find it difficult to change her environment. We all have experienced similar situations. Eventually, after we have exhausted all our options, we might have to find another job. She needs to find an employer and coworkers who will appreciate her skills, attitude, and loyalty. I didn't want her to give up, but the goal at the end of the day is happiness.

- We need to value our positive attitude. If we are not appreciated as employees and managers, then we need to find a better situation.

Chapter 6

The Magic Chemistry for Success: Positive Support and Opportunity, Part 1

Every child is an artist. The problem is how to remain an artist once he grows up.

—Pablo Picasso

My three-year-old daughter, Isabella, bounded out of the restroom in the restaurant. Her mother was right behind her. Isabella had a huge smile on her face. She was very proud of something.

"Daddy, Daddy, I just went tee-tee by myself!" she said proudly and loudly.

I clapped and applauded. Her mother clapped and applauded. Other diners clapped and applauded. It was a true TA DA moment.[1]

When was the last time you went to the bathroom by yourself, walked out, and proudly told the world what you had achieved? Is this not one of the most significant achievements in your life? This is the beginning of independence and self-actualization. How can we work, govern, and create without using the restroom independently and without assistance? If you cannot use the restroom by yourself, you cannot go to preschool. If you cannot attend preschool, you cannot attend elementary, junior high, and high school. You cannot get a job. You cannot work and make a living. The success of the human race depends on the ability of three-year-olds to go to the restroom without assistance. Why not celebrate this achievement when we get older?[2]

A three-year-old has dozens of TA DA moments every day. They cannot wait to tell someone how proud they are of themselves. The parent celebrates every moment. After receiving positive enforcement, they are more confident. Whatever we are celebrating, the three-year-old will do again. And again. And again. And again.[3]

We are just like a three-year-old; we want and expect positive encouragement. Unfortunately, we all want positive support, yet we rarely receive this important treasure or give it out to others. A recent client presented an employee survey at a meeting. One of the questions discussed employees receiving positive support and appreciation for their work and success. More than 50% of the office, according to the client's survey, thought they did not receive positive support. And this is not an isolated issue. When I have a call with a client to discuss their objectives, *every* manager mentions stress, a tough year, a difficult situation, or that the company is dealing with a tremendous amount of change.

I do not have to refer to every report that says people are not happy at their jobs. We get it.

We All Want Two Things: Opportunity and Positive Support

My experience is that we all want two things from our jobs: opportunity and positive support. It does not matter whether we are a CEO, manager, front-line team member, entry level, or intern. We all crave opportunity and positive support as fuel to accomplish our goals. We yearn and wait for someone to tell us that we are appreciated or that we made a difference. When someone finally gives us positive support, we are energized. We walk around as if small forest animals are singing a special tune as they flutter and hop around our bouncing feet. We head to Applebee's for lunch, order appetizers for the table, and rejoice with our potato skins and spinach artichoke dip.

And what happens if we do not receive a little positive support? We sit and wait. We look at the clock. We do the bare minimum. Then we drive home, full of resentment toward our manager wearing the Patagonia vest.

At the beginning of my presentation, I ask everyone to give themselves a round of applause and a TA DA. Many times, the audience looks at me as if I had just asked them to stick a butter knife into their eyeball. They look around to see whether anyone else is going to do it first. I start to encourage the audience members. Finally, they start to applaud. Some groups take to the TA DA immediately. Even in those groups, there are always a few people that half-ass the TA DA. I detest the half-assed TA DA. I call those people out. The audience laughs. We TA DA again, and the audience is more energetic and engaged.

A few minutes later, I then ask them to turn to the people sitting to their right and left, applaud, and tell everyone, "I do a good job here." Again, they give me the butter-knife-in-the-eyeball look. They look around. They look at me. I ask them again to applaud each other. And the audience does it. And they laugh.

Why is giving each other positive support out of our comfort zone? If we cannot get comfortable giving ourselves positive support, how can we give it to the people around us? I have witnessed client events where someone receives an award or an executive mentions a corporate success, and there is no applause. This baffles me. I end up starting the applause, and everyone looks at me asking, "Who is the goofball without a name tag who keeps clapping like a trained seal?" I admit it. I'm an applause starter. I have always started the applause. Sporting events, school performances, award ceremonies, raffles, and every other time more than three people are together, I am known to start the applause.[4] Celebrating birthdays at restaurants are epic applause moments. I am also known to sing "Happy Birthday" in an extremely loud operatic voice that freezes everyone in the entire restaurant, who then breaks out in applause.

The Magic Chemistry for Success: Positive Support and Opportunity

During my presentations, I demonstrate the power of positive support and opportunity with an improvisation exercise. Sometimes the volunteers must answer questions one word at a time. Sometimes the volunteers must act out a series of emotions. Or they must communicate an occupation, location, and object to another audience volunteer without speaking. I am asking the volunteers to work successfully as a team, to be creative, to be accountable, and to effectively communicate. I am asking them to master improvisation after briefly explaining the exercise. The level of difficulty is a double black diamond ski slope during foggy conditions while blindfolded. The volunteers are tentative. Sometimes they can lack confidence. Yet, I believe in each one of them. I know they can succeed. The audience wants them to succeed.

Eventually, the audience volunteer says something. The crowd gives some immediate encouragement through laughter and applause. The volunteer continues by saying or acting out something else in the game. The audience laughs. The volunteer, eyes more confident, shoulders reared back, starts taking more risks and is more productive. The audience responds with more laughter and applause.

This is an incredible visual demonstration of how we *should* work. The more laughter and applause the volunteers receive from the audience, the more productive and creative they are in the game. When each volunteer joins the game, they work together as a team, supporting each other. At this point, the players are receiving positive support from the audience and from each other.

I provided the volunteers with the *opportunity* to create and work together as a team. The audience provided the positive support. It is an amazing chemistry: opportunity and positive support. I have played these exercises thousands of times with thousands of volunteers from all industries. The outcome is always the same. The volunteers are creative, they work effectively as a team, they demonstrate initiative and leadership, they take risks and are creative, and they have fun.

These results are directly related to the magic chemistry of opportunity and positive support.

One more positive support story from an event. This is a story about my absolute favorite and greatest introduction to the stage.

As I previously mentioned, I have spoken at around 2,500 events. And that means I have received 2,500 introductions. I have had some great ones. And I have had some not so great ones. This introduction is about Bob, a conference sponsor who has attended this event for 38 years. Tasked with giving my introduction, he started with a perfect pace and energy. He had the attention of the audience (300–400 people).

One problem. Bob was handed the introduction of yesterday's afternoon speaker, who was a magician. Bob was getting the audience excited about the magician. I was perplexed. Luckily, yesterday's speaker had a long introduction. I motioned to the organization's president and pointed to the stage. He gave me the "everything is fine" hand gesture.

Now what do I do? My microphone was on. I do not remember my exact words, but what I think I said from the side of the ballroom was, "Bob. Bob, you are doing an awesome job with the introduction. But you are reading the introduction for Scotty, yesterday's speaker. I am Joel, today's speaker. Do you think you could read my introduction?"

The audience laughed. I continued. "Bob, I can try to do magic, but I don't think I would be very good." At this point, the president jumps to the stage and gives my introduction to Bob. Bob did not miss a beat. He did not hesitate. He commanded the stage and read my introduction. Bob was incredible. Why? Because I was giving him positive support, and so was the audience.

When I jumped on stage, I said, "Bob, let's make one thing perfectly clear. You were awesome. And it wasn't your fault." The audience loved it. They gave Bob a huge round of applause. And it was an awesome way to introduce my fun and engage the audience.

The Magic Chemistry for Success: Positive Support and Opportunity

After my presentation, many attendees asked whether all this was planned and set up. I promise this was not planned.

I also mentioned Bob in my closing remarks. One of my key messages is about staying in the game. You can do anything you want in improvisation, and you will find success. The only thing you cannot do is quit. You must stay in the game. Bob stayed in the game. And Bob was part of the greatest—and now my favorite—introduction of my career.

Creating a positive environment (just as I did for Bob) and giving each other support and appreciation are easy to accomplish. It takes no budget. We do not have to create a PowerPoint presentation with interlocking circles. We do not have to have a meeting in Orlando. All we need is a few seconds each day to take responsibility and make the right choice. Here are a few ideas to increase the positive support in your office:

- *Be the first person to applaud.* Applause is contagious, whether it is one person saying thank you or a large audience applauding. It only takes one person to start, and within seconds the entire room is cheering. Your team wants to be appreciated. The positive support fuels our passion.

- *Say thank you.* Seems kind of simple, huh? For one day, keep track of how many times you say thank you to your colleagues, partners, vendors, and clients. I think we all would find the results surprising when we realize how few times we say thank you. Guess what. There is no expiration on a thank-you. None. Nobody cares that the thank-you note is late. Why? Because you just made someone's day.

- *Tell people how much you appreciate them.* When was the last time you told a client how much you appreciated their business? When was the last time you told the person sitting next to you?

- *Encourage each other.* Positive support is more than saying thank you. We want the support of the people around us. Support builds confidence. Confidence leads to success and productivity.

- *Help each other achieve success.* Positive support is an action. During an improvisation game the goal is always to help the people around you find success. If they are successful, you are successful.

- *Give significance to awards.* We are rewarding excellence, and in doing so we are also acknowledging, encouraging, and motivating each other. A recent client presented awards for mentoring to some of their employees. A short nomination was read for each winner. The nominations were heartfelt, poignant, and summarized what we all want in a work environment. The awards were presented at the very end of the client's portion of the meeting. They spent the first hour of the meeting talking about the office, work environment, and employee surveys. I told the client they should have given out the awards at the beginning. The awards and the nomination letters are really what we are talking about. As an old journalism professor used to say, "Don't bury the lead," meaning, do not bury what the story is really about in the sixth paragraph. The reason for the story is in the first paragraph. Do not bury the reason for your meeting.

- *Make eye contact when you say thank you.* I play a focus/eye contact game with small groups. It is amazing how difficult it is for people to make eye contact. We look away. We speak to people's foreheads.

- *Make sure they hear you.* When I ask for volunteers to come on stage with me, I want them to know they are in a positive environment. I will prompt the audience to give them several rounds of applause. When they hear the audience applauding,

The Magic Chemistry for Success: Positive Support and Opportunity

they immediately feel more comfortable, and their confidence increases. I know the audience wants the volunteers to achieve success. Good intentions are not enough. The volunteers cannot hear you thinking, "Good luck, Kyle. I hope you do well. Make us proud, Kyle." Applaud each other. Thank each other.

I give my audience volunteers a few minutes of instruction, and they all find success playing the improvisation games. They are successful because of the positive environment. It creates a foundation that allows the volunteers to make the right decisions for success. The same principle that applies to success in the improvisation game will work back at your office.

The other part of the magic chemistry is opportunity, which will be discussed in the next chapter. The key is taking responsibility for your actions and making the choice to create opportunity and positive support in your environment. The results will amaze you.

And if Bob introduces the magician from yesterday instead of you, be ready to give him the positive support he needs.

Quick Ideas

- When you drive home from work, think about all the people you interacted with during the day. Think about the conversations with colleagues, managers, customers, partners, and vendors. Ask yourself, "Did I give the people who deserved it positive support and appreciation?"
- If you did not, then the next day stop by their desk, send an email, send a text, find them on Tinder, or pick up the phone and tell them how much you appreciated their help. Go old-school and write a letter, purchase a stamp, mail the letter, and wait seven business days.

- We all want to hear the words "Thank you" or "I appreciate you." Positive support fuels passion, creativity, teamwork, and leadership. You do not need to have a meeting. You do not need a budget. All you need to do is say, "Thank you." And do not forget there is no expiration date on a thank-you.

The Magic Chemistry for Success: Positive Support and Opportunity

The Magic Chemistry for Success: Positive Support and Opportunity, Part 2

No great man ever complains of want of opportunity.

—Ralph Waldo Emerson

Work is not complicated. To find happiness at work is even less complicated. You know what you really want and need for happiness. I know what you really want and need for happiness. Unfortunately, your manager is clueless.

What if I explained my theory on work happiness in this chapter? What if I could unlock the shrouded mystery of passion, creativity, and fun? If I could explain my theory and help you find your way to happiness, what would you do for me?

I think this information is valuable to individuals and companies. Too many companies have no idea what makes employees happy. It amazes me to see the amount of money companies spend, thinking they are making their employees happy—yet have little to no effect.

Tell me if this sounds familiar: Every year your company has a huge conference in Orlando/San Diego/Las Vegas/Dallas. Each employee or manager is given a name badge and a computer bag/backpack/lighted pen/fleece sweatshirt/quarter-zip emblazoned with logos. Employees shuffle into a large conference room and are shown PowerPoint slides of upside-down triangles/interlocking circles/multicolored bar graphs about the past year. The conference theme is called Elevate or has something to do with everyone climbing a mountain/finishing a race/ blasting off to new sales goals/surviving in a jungle. Attendees then eat chicken for lunch.

After lunch, everyone builds a boat/car/rocket ship from cardboard/ paper towels/aluminum foil, with the winners receiving Starbucks/ Best Buy/Chili's gift certificates. They eat beef/shrimp/salmon at a gala dinner and are presented awards for sales competitions/longevity with the company/doing their job. Afterward, the employees watch a comedian/juggler/hypnotist. Everyone, bleary-eyed from late night drinks, flies home in the morning.

The motivation lasts about a week. Employees and managers go back to their jobs and settle into the same routines. They have the same stress and frustrations. Employees do not change how they work, manage, or communicate.

Nobody has figured out what they need for long-term happiness. Nobody has even asked whether the employees were happy. The company thinks, "Hey, I just took you to Orlando, and we built a damn rocket ship together. Everyone seemed like they were having fun. Yep, all is well here."

Okay, if I am going to translate the Rosetta stone of work happiness, you need to do something for me. They are simple requests, yet they could change the course of humanity. Some of these requests might seem difficult for you to grant, but we all need to pull together.

My requests:

- Stop describing your product/company/service as "world-class" or "state-of-the-art." State-of-the-art lasts about 60 days, and what does "world-class" really mean? Are you really that proud that you are kicking French Guiana's ass?

- Stop scheduling Zoom calls at 8 a.m. I work from home. Usually, I shower and dress by around 11 a.m. It is currently 9:41 a.m. as I write this. Yep, I still have not showered.

- Does everything have to be a Zoom or Teams video call? Can we just call each other?

- Stop saying, "We are going in a different direction." If you chose a different person for the job, a different vendor for the project, or something else, then say that.

- Stop speeding up when I am trying to merge my car into your lane. For the love of God, would it kill you to acknowledge my blinker and let me in?

- Stop taking off your shoes on airplanes. The flight is two hours long; put your paws back in the loafers. Speaking of loafers, if you are a man, please stop wearing loafers without socks.

- Stop serving iced tea that is not brewed.

- Stop trying to sell me the warranty. The odds are small that I will remember that I have a warranty, or even know where I filed the paperwork. I once purchased a vacuum warranty. Who does that? Have I used the three free vacuum cleanings that probably cost $49.95? Nope. You want to prove that I am an idiot? Easy. Show the jury the vacuum warranty.

- Stop using the word "silo." As in, "We need to work together more effectively as a team, because we currently are working in silos." Does anyone really know what this means? Does this have to do with the wheat harvest in Kansas or the nuclear missiles in Kansas?

- Stop creating acronyms for event themes and initiatives to motivate attendees, or to educate employees.

- **S**illy **T**hemes **O**ffend **P**eople.

Okay, are you ready for the key? I may have mentioned this once or twice, but it's kind of important.

We only want two things from our jobs:

1. Opportunity.

2. Positive support.

That's it. The hard part is that we all want different opportunities. Some of us want the opportunity to manage or lead. Some of us want the opportunity to present and use new ideas. Some want the opportunity to help people. Some want a different role or responsibility, or more training, or the opportunity to attend a conference.

How do you know what opportunity you need? Be honest. Ask yourself, "What is going to make me fulfilled and rewarded at work?" It is not more money. We all want more money. Yet that happiness only lasts to the next paycheck, and we are right back where we started: not passionate about our work and not fulfilled.

When you are honest with yourself, the answer will surprise you. You will understand what opportunity you need to be fulfilled at work. The next surprise is when you tell your manager. A great manager will realize how easy it is to provide you opportunity. What do they get back in return? A motivated team member that will help them reach their goals.

And if the manager refuses to give you the opportunity that you requested? You just received a huge clue that you are in the wrong place. That is okay. There are plenty of other companies who will jump at the chance to hire a passionate and energized team member that will help them find success.

And then we want someone to say thank you. Simple, huh? This is what work is all about: opportunity and positive support. In every industry I have spoken to, every level of employee and manager craves opportunity and positive support from their jobs. Think about every job you have ever had. You may have not realized it, but you left that job because you did not receive the opportunity or positive support you needed.

The sad part is that we all *want* opportunity and positive support to fuel our passion, creativity, and success, yet we do not receive enough. We do not give enough opportunity and positive support to our team, colleagues, customers, partners, or vendors. Guess what happens when our managers refuse to provide opportunity and positive support? We are not happy. We come to work every day physically, but mentally we are gone. Bye-bye.

We meet bye-bye people all the time. They walk among us. They do not care about their job. They don't care about the company. And they certainly don't care about you. Ever get a grumpy customer service person? Bye-bye. Need help with scheduling a repair? Bye-bye. Need some help from another department? Bye-bye.

Bye-bye people whine. Bye-bye people bitch. Bye-bye people are not pleasant people to hang out with during the annual holiday party. Eventually, bye-bye people realize why they are not happy. They quit and find another job. The rest of the office rejoices when the bye-bye person leaves. Unfortunately, those rejoicing have to pick up bye-bye's work until they hire another person, train that person, and get that person up to speed. More work for those rejoicing. More stress for those rejoicing. All of a sudden, one person rejoicing becomes a bye-bye, and the story starts again.

How do we stop this circle of life?

Your clueless manager is not going to just give out opportunity, because they are afraid someone is going to make a mistake. And your manager is correct. We are all going to make mistakes. We want to minimize mistakes. We want to learn from our mistakes. We are not going to eliminate mistakes.

Sometimes You Ask for Opportunity, Sometimes You Take Opportunity, and Sometimes You Demand Opportunity

If the clueless manager refuses to give you opportunity, go into their office, sit in the chair opposite their desk that is the size of a regulation pool table, look at their autographed football, and ask for the opportunity. Explain to your manager that opportunity is what drives you. Opportunity makes you happy.

If you are a manager, when was the last time you asked your team what they want? Have you taken the time to ask what makes them happy? Ask yourself, "Have I given them an opportunity?" "Have I taken away an opportunity because I thought the employee would make a mistake?"

Now, match the opportunity with positive support. All of a sudden, there is a magical chemistry. Positive support and feedback build confidence. The employee has ownership and responsibility. Do you know what happens when a team member or manager has ownership and responsibility? They start to care. Do you know what happens when people start to care? They have passion. See? It really is simple.

I am amazed every time I give audience volunteers the opportunity to perform an improvisation game during my keynote. After every presentation, an executive will say a version of, "I cannot believe Kevin from accounting acted as a ballerina." Kevin twirled. Kevin jumped. I *knew* Kevin would be an awesome ballerina. I *gave* Kevin the opportunity. The audience *gave* him positive support. Just give people opportunity and step back. Take away the fear that someone will micromanage them, and they blossom. Opportunity is magical.

Everyone wants to play. Everyone wants to laugh. We just lack the opportunity to play. Providing that opportunity during my keynote proves my point. We are starving our team members of opportunity. Or we starve them of positive support.

The worst action is giving a team member opportunity but micromanaging so much that you soul-crush them. Sometimes my audience volunteers are incredible performers. Sometimes there is beautiful chaos. The volunteer is making choices that are not working. My job is to create support through opportunity so the audience member finds success. If I micromanage, they will become disheartened and quit the game. Sometimes we must accept beautiful chaos.

Let me break it down into three steps:

1. Create opportunity by allowing team members and managers to have ownership and responsibility. Let them create and work without micromanaging them.

2. Once an employee or manager has ownership, they start to care. Do you care about anything without some form of ownership or responsibility?

3. Caring turns into passion. Again, do you have passion for anything that you don't care about?

Your employees are creative and passionate. They want to do good work and make the company successful. All they need is opportunity and positive support.

And if you do not believe me, just watch Kevin twirl around as a ballerina at your Elevate conference in Orlando right before the chicken is served.

Quick Ideas

The next time you have a great experience at work take five minutes and reflect on your day. Write down everything that happened to you that day.

- Why was today so rewarding?

- Why was today a great day at work?

- What did you do?

- What did people say to you?

- What did your manager say and do?

Now, you have an exact list of what you need for happiness. Now, work toward achieving the goals on that list every day.

- Speak with your manager about the list. Ask for opportunities. You know what you need to be happy, productive, and effective.

- Be part of the process.

You cannot hope the same circumstances that made one day perfect will magically happen again. You can, however, work toward the circumstances that created the happiness. You must demand opportunity and positive support.

Chapter 8

The Five TA DA Tenets of Teamwork

Always do right; this will gratify some people and astonish the rest.

—Mark Twain

If you want to lift yourself up, lift up someone else.

—Booker T. Washington

We all want to be awesome team players. A normal and sane person (and this includes almost all of us) does not wake up in the morning, dress for work, eat breakfast, and say, "I am going to be negative today. I am going to whine. I am not going to work well with others. I will probably eat someone's blueberry muffin in the break room." Your colleagues do not get in the car and head to work planning on being a terrible teammate.[1]

We do not become *great* teammates because there is no foundation for *great* teamwork. As leaders, we must create the opportunity and foundation for our team to excel, produce, and create. If we create the right foundation, great teamwork will happen.

I use improvisation to discuss the foundation and right choices for successful teamwork. I have watched thousands of diverse audience members perform on stage in front of their peers. I give a few moments of instruction. The team is creative, focused, supportive, meets their goals and objectives, takes responsibility, is accountable, and most important, has fun.

The foundation I create for audience volunteers who share the stage with me is the same foundation we must create as leaders. Here is the best part. It is simple. If I can create this foundation on stage in front of an audience in only a few minutes, you can do this at your work.

This chapter covers the tenets of teamwork that I have learned watching thousands of audience volunteers perform with me on stage. The audience volunteers *all* make the same choices in how they work together to overcome challenges and meet the objectives. In an earlier chapter, I discussed the importance of leaders to create the opportunity for great teamwork. Once the opportunity is created, team members must *make* the right choices to find success.

First, I want to share a story. During a recent event, I was playing a game I call Road Trip. Three audience volunteers join me on stage. From the audience, I ask for a road trip destination and four emotions (I am also participating in the game). Each audience volunteer is assigned an emotion. As the "driver" picks up each hitchhiker, everyone must take on the emotion of the last person who entered the car. The driver then drops off the hitchhikers in order, and the group changes their emotion in reverse.

At a recent event, I did something different. I asked the audience for a story to go along with the road trip. Something that happened to them on a recent car ride. A man in the front told a story about driving the back roads of Arkansas and not being able to find a restroom. He stopped at an abandoned gas station. As he relieved himself, he noticed giant rats were all around him.[2] We call this comedy gold.

I asked my team to try and incorporate the story into our road trip. During the improv game (in front of more than 1,000 people), the volunteers mentioned driving through Arkansas, having to go to the bathroom, and not seeing anywhere to stop. The participants incorporated the story *and* continued to change their emotions. I was elated at the incredible teamwork. The audience laughed and applauded. And then the team, buoyed by the audience's positive support, made a choice that demonstrated even more amazing teamwork. Two of the audience members exited the car (as they were instructed) and walked to the back of the stage. Backs to the audience, arms around each other, they acted (tastefully) like they were relieving themselves. The audience went nuts. Building on their idea, I jumped on the chair, acted like a giant rat, and scurried around the stage.[3] I am certain not one attendee who walked into their ballroom that morning expected to see their keynote speaker acting like a giant rat as two audience members (again, tastefully and backs to the audience) implied that they were relieving themselves.

The audience volunteers created a magical improvisational moment. They worked together as a team. They were creative. They were accountable and took ownership. They listened and supported each other. Isn't that what we all want from our teams? I provided the opportunity. They made the choices, on their own, that led to successful teamwork.

Let us examine five of their choices. They are the five TA DA tenets of teamwork:

1. **Be open and flexible.** We all have different backgrounds, educations, and experiences. We work differently. We think differently. And we all have our own ways to solve problems. To me, a variety of perspectives is an advantage.

   The secret to making this work is your choice of openness and flexibility. If you are a "my way or the highway" type of person, you are going to struggle in the team environment.

The Five TA DA Tenets of Teamwork

You are also not going to have many friends that will help you move when you get divorced.

When I use improvisation games to demonstrate my messages, the audience members who perform best will accept each other's ideas, and work to make the idea better. They are open to new ideas. And they accept and are flexible to how their teammates are participating.

We will make mistakes. Our teammates will choose different paths than we prefer. We can choose to be frustrated. Or we can choose to be open and flexible.

We must answer the first question of improvisation, "How do I help the other people around me be successful?" We should all ask and act on that question. To make that question really work, we must be open and flexible to ideas and how people work and engage.

When the first audience volunteer left the car on the road trip, the second followed him. One person had the idea to go to the back of the stage. The other volunteer was open and flexible to the idea and reacted. The first volunteer put his arm around the other. The second did the same. That moment, because of the teamwork, elicited a huge laugh from the audience. His openness and flexibility created that moment. What if he fought the idea? He might have defeated the volunteer with the idea, and the moment would never have happened. Instead, he reacted positively and even built on the idea.

2. **Solicit and encourage the team to give ideas.** Sometimes people on the team do not want to participate. When I bring an audience member on stage that is reticent, I immediately ask a question. "Where do they live?" "What is their job?" This forces my teammate to respond and engage. The audience

will usually give them some positive encouragement, and the audience volunteer starts to build confidence. The confidence builds during the game. They take more risks. The audience gives more positive support.

The same is true for your teams. People want to voice their opinions and ideas. Create the opportunity for the team to contribute to the plan. Remember to be open to their ideas.

When you ask for ideas, the reality is that few of the ideas will ever be used. That is the nature of creativity. As a leader, the most important action is to reward and appreciate the team member's time spent creating the idea. We want the team to continue to produce ideas. If we reward the time and energy creating the ideas, the team member will be engaged and want to produce more ideas.

The nature of improvisation is that everyone on stage contributes. Everyone has an opportunity to create. All three audience volunteers contributed in the Road Trip game. The audience rewarded them with laughter and applause. The positive support led to the idea of going to the back of the stage. And it led to me imitating a giant rat.[4]

3. **Create ownership and responsibility.** We all want our team to be passionate about our goals, work, customers, and mission. People do not always walk into a room beaming with passion. If they do, you might want to ask for a drug test.

Passion happens with a chemical equation. The first step is creating ownership and responsibility. When the team has ownership of the idea, plan, execution, goals, or any other part, they start to care. We do not care about anything unless we have ownership and responsibility. Once the team cares about something, then there is passion. We do not have passion for something unless we first care about it. Everything starts with ownership and responsibility.

I want the audience volunteers on stage to participate and take ownership. I am there to support them and make sure they are successful. However, it is as much their exercise as it is mine. As a leader, sometimes we want to do everything. We want to take control. Sometimes we think, "It is not going to get done unless I do it." And that could be true. How do you know if you do not ever give your team the ownership and responsibility? It is hard to let go. The reward, though, is seeing your team engaged and producing.

The audience volunteers in the Road Trip game all took ownership. They wanted the team to succeed. They supported each other, built on each other's ideas, and contributed to the team's success.

4. **Focus on the plan and act.** Once we give the team ownership and responsibility, we need to quickly focus on the goal and act. If we shorten the time frame of our goal, we force the team to focus. The longer we must act, the more time we will overanalyze, lose focus, or lose track.

Shorten the time frames and force the team to focus. When we take too long to decide, the team will feel less engaged. They will start to drift and lose confidence in the team.

Improvisation forces you to focus on the team and objective. In another chapter, I discussed the concept of being "in the moment." That focus allows the team to understand what everyone needs to be successful. The team engages with each other because everyone is overcoming the immediate challenge of the game.

Improvisation is built on quickly choosing an idea and everyone focusing and acting to make that idea work. How can you take that back to your work? Can you shorten the time frames? Can you engage the team more on the objective? Can you create more positive support?

Value the team's contribution, and they will engage. Communicate through the process, and allow each team member ownership. When I perform with audience members, I only explain the game and the rules. I do not tell them what they should do during the game. They make their own choices. That freedom empowers the team members. Nobody wants a micromanager. Nobody wants a leader who says, "I would have done it this way."

A leader must empower their team to focus on the challenge, take ownership, and contribute. Each audience volunteer made these choices throughout the Road Trip game.

5. **Be positive and supportive.** The best gift you can ever give your team is positive support and appreciation. It is their fuel. Everyone wants to be appreciated. When you go home from work, think about all the people on the team. Did you give the team members encouragement, appreciation, and positive support? If not, then do it tomorrow. Send an email. Call them on the phone. Say something in the hall.

There is no expiration date on appreciation and support. It is not a ham.

When I bring audience members on stage to perform an improvisation game, I make sure they have three rounds of applause before they even start the game. Once the participants start engaging, the audience will laugh and applaud. The more positive support they receive, the more creative and productive they are in the game.

Part of a successful team is the reduction of ego. One element of being positive and supportive is sharing credit in our

73

accomplishments. Once the team understands that everyone is dependent on each other's success, they focus more on the goal. As a leader, share the credit with your team.

These five choices all contributed to the success of the Road Trip game. The cool part is that the art form of improvisation forced the volunteers to make these choices. You must make these choices to succeed in improvisation.

When you go to work, nobody is forcing you to make these choices. There is not an audience laughing and applauding and creating confidence. You make these choices. And if you do make these choices, you will be amazed at how your team functions. I also hope you remember a road trip through the back roads of Arkansas and giant rats.

Chapter 9

The Foundation for Teamwork: Making Everyone Else Successful

Individual commitment to a group effort—that is what makes a team work, a company work, a society work, a civilization work.

—Vince Lombardi

We have corrupted the phrase "team building." Too often, team building means a time on the agenda when we have nothing planned, so we rush something together at the last minute. Anytime two or more people get together and do an activity, somebody is calling it team building. We may drink margaritas. We may have a guacamole-making contest. We may build boats with paper towel tubes, wax paper, and cotton balls on a beach in Florida. All of this is fun. I am just not sure we are building a team.

Most team building events are really happiness-building events. When the vice president of Global International Sales takes the team to a resort to play golf and/or have a spa day, they do not really plan on working on any skills to increase team effectiveness. The vice president *does* want to make the team happy. And a happy team, the VP thinks, will work harder. The VP is happiness building.

You attend the annual meeting with the theme of "Engage" or "Elevate." Then you engage in a scavenger hunt/cross the volcanic lava river/build a spaghetti tower/build a marshmallow tower/ build a spaghetti and marshmallow tower combo game. Do these games really address how to make a team more effective or productive? Team members are spending time together without the pressures of day-to-day work. All of these activities are fun. And they certainly can build mutual respect, camaraderie, and encourage friendships. Again, the employees are happiness building.

I love happiness building. Most employees and managers would probably have a better attitude about the activity if we called it happiness building. Mention "team building" and people always crunch up their face, audibly sigh, and make comments about the "silliness" of the activity. Do you know how many times an attendee has said to me, "I hate team building, but I had fun during your workshop"? I have seen too many clients start an activity, and then attendees complain and mope around with a bad attitude because they do not like the words "team building." Guess what. Within 10 minutes, those same attendees are having a blast. Do you know why? Because a scavenger hunt in San Antonio beats the hell out of spending the day processing, manufacturing, selling, distributing, developing, managing, or synergizing. Team building is basically recess for adults. Sometimes, the adults even get to play with a ball. Nobody would pay for recess if we called it happiness building. Or, for that matter, if we just called it recess. I have said it many times: "Everyone wants to play." Create the right foundation and opportunity for play, and attendees will jump at the chance to build something with spaghetti.

School children get recess at least once a day. Adults get an official recess from work once or twice a year. Some adults have been known to create their own independent, unsanctioned, and unofficial recess. If they are inclusive, legal, respectful, and have everyone's best interest in mind, I am all for independent, unsanctioned, and unofficial recesses.

We need happiness building, and we need to have it often—maybe not every day, but often. Happiness building creates your work culture. It creates a sense of shared community. Creating surprises and fun should always be a pillar of your work culture.

What We Also Need Is Team Effectiveness

Team effectiveness is much different than team building. You have already built your team, so again the term "team building" is incorrect. What you are now trying to do now is make your team more effective, productive, and successful. We spend so much time building boats, playing golf, and having scavenger hunts that we forget to actually discuss how we can work together more effectively.

What makes an effective and productive team? Every chapter in this book covers some aspect of a successful team. You just have to apply the messages. I think good teamwork in improvisation and in work comes down to two basic principles:

1. *Take responsibility for your role and do the best job possible.*

2. *Help everyone else achieve success.*

Sometimes we make effective teamwork too complicated. It is not. As I have stated many times, the same principles that apply to improvisation will apply to your job. If you want to work on team effectiveness, then work on these two principles.

During my presentations, I like to keep the concept of teamwork simple. The best message improvisation taught me about teamwork:

1. Ask the question: "How do I help the people around me be more successful?" This is the easy part.

2. Answer the question. You are smart. You know what your colleagues, customers, partners, and vendors need to be successful.

3. Act on the answer. This is the hard part. This is what makes a great company.

If you are reading this book, I hope you have seen a live improvisation comedy show. After every performance, someone always asks me, "How does it work?" The audience member wants to understand how a team of performers can work so well together without a script, plan, or rehearsal.

We are asking the above question, answering it, and acting on the answer. Successful improvisation is not about being the star, or the funniest person on stage. Each performer actively chooses to make their teammates look great. They are asking the question, answering it, and acting on it.

Acting on the information is really the hard part. This defines the great companies. These are the companies that appear on "the best places to work" lists. And the best part: when you help the people around you be successful, the reward is significant. Who do we help? We tend to help the people that have helped us. We notice these things.

Take Responsibility for Your Role and Do the Best Job Possible

One improvisation game I use is called One-Line Story. I start with two audience members who are placed at opposite ends of the stage. One of the volunteers creates the beginning sentence for our story. The participant at the other end of the stage must improvise the last line of our story. I then ask four or five people from the audience to come on stage and add one line to the story. They can enter and add their line at the beginning, middle, or end. It doesn't matter. We then retell the story. I repeat the process. Add four or five lines and retell the story. We do this until we have a complete story or run out of audience members.

Each person has one line in the story. It is up to each participant to take responsibility for their one line. They can use their line to make a transition, add a detail, or to take the story in another direction. Volunteers can add lines randomly and out of sequence. It is up to the next group of volunteers to incorporate each line and create a story. Because each volunteer has only one line, they need to take responsibility for their one line.

The story really works when participants help each other to tell a better story. When they listen to each other and add lines that support, help, or build the story, everyone succeeds. For the game to really work, participants must take responsibility and ask, "What can I do to make the story better?" The volunteers decide where to add their line so they can help fill a hole in the story, answer a question, or make another participant's random line fit.

Help Everyone Else Achieve Success

When was the last time you were at work and thought, *How do I help the people around me achieve more success?* True teamwork is consistently asking this question. Creating effective teamwork is not complicated. I think it really comes down to taking responsibility and asking this question every day. Successful teams will ask this question. Every moment I am on stage as an improviser, I want the other players to succeed. I want to help them be productive and effective. If my colleagues are successful, I am going to be successful.

Some people waste their one line because they don't listen, don't care, or use their one line to try and get the big laugh at the expense of the story. And, of course, when that happens, the story never works. I had a group once where every line was a random, independent thought. Not one line made any sense because nobody was trying to help the other players. Not one person was taking responsibility. Nobody was listening. Nobody was helping. It was one big bowl of desperation chili.

We all have one line in many stories. We have the story of our job, our family, organizations, hobbies, sports, and friends. What are you doing with your one line? Have you given your best effort? Are you making the story better? Are you using your one line to help, create, or lead? Are you making others successful? If you are unable to figure out what you are doing with your one line, then you need to reassess what you want to accomplish and make some changes.

Yes, we have only one line in a huge story. Guess what. That one line is very powerful. In the improvisation game, one line can change the entire story. One line can help everyone achieve success. And, just as in the One-Line Story game, every story starts with one line.

How Do I Help the People around Me Achieve More Success?

I never tell the participants what they have to do with their one line in the story. And I never tell them where they have to go in the story. Each participant has to take initiative. When the participants join the group on stage, they are excited. You can see their energy rise. They want to make sure they are joining the story in the right place, contributing something worthwhile, and creating a better story. There is excitement and passion in their actions. When they were in the audience, they were enjoying the game, but were still not owners in the process. Their attitude changed once they joined the story. They now want the story to be successful.

I could easily tell everyone who comes on stage where to stand and say their line. I could even give them their line. Do you think they would have as much fun? Do you think they would enjoy the process as much—or at all? I have created the opportunity for them to succeed. I have to allow them to take initiative and ownership of the game. Sure, they might make a mistake. We all make mistakes. We want to minimize mistakes and learn from them, but we can't be afraid to take the risk. They will learn. And the next group will help them be successful.

A successful team cares about the outcome. They have to be passionate about what is happening to the team. If they don't care, they are not passionate. Seems like a simple solution, huh? You have to create the opportunity for the team to take initiative and ownership. As each person becomes involved, they want the story to succeed. The participants realize their success is dependent on the other people playing the game. One line is very powerful, and it can turn the story. One line can help other lines. The audience might only remember your line. Still, you need everyone else to make your one line a success.

My Success Is Dependent on Your Success

There is one more aspect of the game I want to discuss. Some lines in the story may have nothing to do with other lines, yet they are still dependent on each other. If you work for a big company, you may never speak to some of the managers and employees in the other offices. Still, their success is dependent on your success. We are still under the same brand. We have to think about everyone on our team, not just the people sitting next to us. Either everyone is going to be successful in an improvisation game or everyone is going to fail. And that applies to business as well. It is not just one or two members of the team finding success. Everyone on the team creates success. And to me, that is what team effectiveness is all about.

The game works because:

1. Participants want the team to succeed.
2. Participants have the courage to get out of their comfort zone and help the team.
3. Participants take responsibility for their role. They also understand how their role benefits the team.

4. Participants are encouraging others. Each time someone adds a line, the story improves, and the team succeeds.

5. Participants have the latitude to make mistakes. They know another teammate will be there to help their line make sense and improve the story.

6. Each participant is an equal. And each participant's contribution is valued.

You have to want to create a successful team and take responsibility. Remember to ask the most important question: *"How do I help the people around me be more successful?"* Your answer will determine your actions and direct you to the right path.

Now, who wants to build a spaghetti and marshmallow tower for some happiness building?

Quick Ideas

I think a big part of team effectiveness is communicating what needs to change to achieve success. This is rarely done during the common team-building activities that seem to occur at every meeting. I have a solution. This is an easy game that can produce an effective dialogue within your group and also generate substantial ideas.

If you have a large group, split them into teams of 6–10 people. Ask your team what challenges they would like to discuss. Give each team a flip chart and one of the challenges. Here are some examples of challenges I have seen from my clients:

- How can we communicate more effectively among departments?

- How do we increase morale and have more fun and passion at work?

- How do we create a better work-life balance?

- How do we work together more effectively?

   Ask each team to write down the challenge they will discuss on the flip chart. Each group must work together to come up with as many ideas as possible to meet the challenge. Try to have the teams develop ideas that employees or managers can accomplish on a daily/weekly basis, a monthly basis, and a yearly basis. Remember, this is a creative time. Do not analyze your ideas right now. A facilitator should move around the room to remind the groups not to spend time discussing and debating ideas. Use the time to generate ideas.

- Give the group 20–30 minutes to generate ideas. Bring all of the teams back together and discuss the ideas. If you have time, you can talk about all of the ideas. If you are short on time, ask the group to pick out their best. This is the time to analyze. Encourage dialogue among all participants.

- If you really want to put some of these ideas to work, nominate a captain for each group. The captain is responsible for sending out an email with each team's ideas and for working toward making some of the ideas a reality.

- After the exercise, serve cookies. Cookies are an important and often overlooked ingredient to team effectiveness.

The Foundation for Teamwork: Making Everyone Else Successful

The Secrets to Success During Change and Disruption: Embrace the Chaos; Be Open and Flexible; Be in the Moment; Be Prepared for Change

I get up every morning determined to both change the world and have one hell of a good time. Sometimes this makes planning my day difficult.

—E. B. White

I do not speak behind a lectern.[1] They are large, cumbersome, and create a barrier between the audience and speaker. When there is a lectern, I always ask the client to move it off the stage to create more space to play the improvisation exercises. I have learned something very important in my speaking career: People do not like to move the lectern. I am not talking about physically moving it. That is fairly easy. It is the idea that there will be a "change" by moving it. The change kills them. The stage manager or client will look at me as though I'd asked them if I could borrow their car to enter a demolition derby next week in Missouri. People do not like change.

Like most changes, moving the lectern is not important. We only assign importance to the act of moving it. Nobody in the audience really cares where the lectern is located on the stage. I am sure an attendee has never written on their meeting evaluation, "I didn't like the lectern placement, but the juggling hypnotist was awesome."[2]

The issue is that I am changing their decision. I once had a client who refused to move the lectern (which was placed center stage). I explained that I do not speak from behind a lectern and that I use improvisation games that tend to work better if I am in the middle of the stage where the audience can see me. "Nope, we just cannot move the lectern," he said. "A vice president is going to speak after your program, and he rehearsed with the lectern," the client explained.

"Can we ask the vice president if we can move the lectern?" Nope. He is a vice president, I was told. He is a very important person. In what kind of world do we live where the vice president of International GlobalCom InfoDataVerse Solutions (not the company's real name) is so untouchable that a mere commoner such as I could possibly ask him if we could move the lectern? I casually walked up and spoke with the vice president. Sit down for the big reveal: he did not care about the location of the lectern, so it was moved. Also, true story, the same vice president came on stage dressed as a Roman gladiator/emperor/soldier. I am not sure how the outfit relates to change, but it still makes me laugh.[3]

You see, not only does removing the lectern involve changing a prior decision; it now involves work. The point of the story is that people do not like change, and they do not like moving stuff. Ask your friends to come over and help you move your house. Watch the reaction. Nobody wants to move anything. And nobody likes change.

Of course, we end up moving the lectern. And then, after I am finished speaking, a stressed-out person moves the lectern back for the vice president. And then the vice president of International GlobalCom InfoDataVerse Solutions walks on stage, does not go anywhere near the lectern, and thanks everyone for coming to the meeting. He does not even walk close enough to the lectern to touch the damn thing. He speaks for about 97 seconds.[4]

Change Is Scary. The Idea of Change Is Even Scarier

We all fear change. Change represents something unknown. We might have to learn something new. We might have to leave our comfort zone. We might even have to change the way we work. We prefer to curl up in our warm Pottery Barn blanket and dismiss or ignore change. It does not matter. Change will happen. We will never arrive at work one day and hear someone say, "Okay, we are all done changing here at International GlobalCom InfoDataVerse Solutions." Cool. I knew it would happen on a Tuesday. This really frees up the rest of the week. Can we order pizza?

Improvisation taught me four important lessons to succeed during change:

1. Be prepared for change.
2. Be open and flexible to change.
3. Embrace change.
4. Be in the moment during change.

All the improvisation games I use highlight these lessons. For this discussion, I want to discuss a game called Know-it-All. I invite three audience members to come on stage and answer questions. The key is the volunteers can only say one word at a time, in order of how they are standing, to complete the sentence. The three players have to listen, support each other, and work together to create a sentence. Like all improvisation games, there is constant change and disruption. And the only way the game works is if everyone is prepared for change, is open and flexible to change, is a great listener, and embraces change.

Be Prepared for Change

When I ask audience volunteers to join me on stage, they make their first choice as they get up from their seat. They are choosing to be prepared for change. They have no idea what game I am going to play, their role or responsibility, or what will happen during the game.

They choose to prepare for change. Huge. Preparing for change will set their tone, approach, energy, and attitude. They understand change will happen. The volunteers have embraced change. The change and disruption will not surprise them, frustrate them, stress them out, or create impatience.

Be Open and Flexible to Change

Change is going to happen whether we like it or not. Most change is completely out of our control. We only control how we react to it. Too many times we even give up control of how we react to change. Would you really choose to be stressed or frustrated? No, you would not. Choosing how you react to change determines your attitude, approach, and success. We choose to be open and flexible. We choose to be helpful, patient, supportive, and understanding.

We all have different backgrounds, experiences, skills, and education. We will not all solve the problem the same way. Our differences make us a stronger team. We each see the problem through a different lens. We must be open and flexible to each other's ideas. That flexibility allows us to build on the idea, and grow and expand the idea.

Embrace Change

Improvisation teaches you to embrace change. You never know what will happen because there is no script, no plan, and no rehearsal.

Just by adjusting how you approach change, you determine your attitude.

Improvisation is constant chaos and disruption. I have no idea what the other performer will say and do. Embracing change will force you to trust your abilities, it creates confidence, and makes you more aware of the situation. It does not mean all change is right or good. Some change sucks. Some change does not work. Embracing just means we understand change is going to happen. We can then decide how to move forward with the change.

Be in the Moment During Change

Choosing to embrace change forces you to be more present and in the moment. You have a heightened sense of awareness because you want to react and produce success. When you are in the moment, you focus on the game, the team, and the objective. You are truly listening and not waiting for your turn to speak. Being in the moment makes you a better leader, teammate, communicator, and innovator. You are more productive.

I have played Know-it-All thousands of times. Some people do not listen to each other, and the game does not work. Some people try to anticipate what word is coming next, and the game does not work. Some people try to project what they want the other person to say, and the game does not work. The game works only when each player listens and reacts with openness and flexibility, embraces change, prepares for change, and is present. You will never know what word is coming next or where the sentence is headed. Just like your job, you never know what issue or challenge will surface next. It is impossible to know.

And how do we react to change? Most of the time our first reaction to change is frustration, impatience, and stress. We are not preparing ourselves for change. The surprise of change creates the frustration. We know change is going to happen. I live in Texas. It's hot in Texas. I know the air conditioner will crash almost every summer right about the time Texas reaches the same temperature as the surface of the sun. I call the air conditioner repairman. He comes out two days later. He will need a part to fix the air conditioner. The part will arrive next week, he tells me. So, each summer, my wife and I sit around sweating as if we were unloading big rigs at a warehouse in hell. And every summer during this intense passion play, I am frustrated, impatient, and stressed. I know the change is coming. I am just not very open and flexible when I am sweating off my eyebrows.

Change Is Going to Happen—We Might as Well Be Open and Flexible

We all know we have to deal with change at our jobs. You will suffer growing pains under new management. You will have to learn a new software program. The company will introduce a new "state-of-the-art, world-class" product that will kick the competition's ass in French Guiana. Someone is going to move your desk from the cubicle by the window to the corner near the bathroom. The same corner that has an average midday temperature of 32° Fahrenheit. There will be new competition, there will be an economic downturn, supply chain issues, someone will make a mistake, something will break—there will always be something. How we deal with change determines our stress and passion, and plays a role in our leadership, communication, and creativity. If we do not manage our stress, we lose our passion. We deflate. We wallow. We mope.

One of the interesting lessons I learned from the Know-it-All game is that either the whole team will achieve success or the whole team will fail. Success cannot happen to only one or two people in the game. Either everyone is going to meet the objective and create a sentence that makes sense or the team will struggle. This is an important lesson. Our success is dependent on each other's success. We must help each other. The whole object of the Know-it-All game is to answer the question as a team, working together for a common cause. Sounds familiar, huh?

Again, improvisation forces the players to make the right decision to meet the objective. It forces the team to listen, to be open and flexible, and to help each other create the sentence.

Most of the change that causes stress we end up forgetting in a short time. It might be a few days. It might be a few hours. Our mind realizes the change is not that important. Why cannot we figure this out when the change occurs? If we can direct our energy toward things that really matter, we could reduce our stress.

Ask Two Simple Questions to Manage Change

We have to manage our change. I deal with change by asking myself two simple questions:

1. Does the change affect my ability to be happy and successful in my job?

2. Does the change affect the ability of those around me—my family, colleagues, clients, and vendors—to be happy and successful in their jobs?

If both answers are no, then I know the change is not that important. I can direct my energy and passion toward something that does affect my success and happiness. Trouble starts creeping up on our shoulders when we spend too much time and energy on actions and words outside these two questions. Ask yourself these two questions. Really, everything that truly matters is covered by these two questions.

Sometimes after I play Know-it-All, I ask the audience to pair up and play the two-person version of the game. I ask them to find another pair and have a conversation one word at a time. After the game, I ask the audience how they dealt with openness and flexibility. The answer is always the same: they listened to each other. Pretty simple, huh? If for one second during the game, they stop listening or look at something shiny in the room, the game fails. They must listen and work in the moment.

Let us think about what happens when each player listens:

- The players meet their objective and create a sentence that makes sense.
- The players become more creative and confident.
- The players work together as a team.
- The players communicate successfully.
- The players take responsibility and show initiative.
- The players have fun.

If I asked any manager what they wanted from their team, do you think the manager would list anything different? This is what we want from each other. The foundation to that success is always the same thing: listening. When I tell my audiences that we all must listen more actively, everyone nods in approval: "Yes, we must all listen better. He is right. He is not talking about me, but others in this room definitely need to listen better." We *all* need to listen better.

Change is going to happen every day. We have to deal with change in a productive manner that allows us to stay passionate, creative, and energized. If we spend all day frustrated and stressed, we will have no fuel for our happiness. We can manage change. We can reduce our stress and at the same time increase our passion. Remember the secrets of the Know-it-All game: Embrace change, be open and flexible during change, be prepared for change, and be in the moment during change.

And, finally, just move the damn lectern.

Quick Ideas

Take a few minutes and think about your last week at work. Now, make a list and write down everything that caused frustration, impatience, and stress. After you have completed your list, try and read it with a straight face. You cannot. You are giggling too much.

Certainly, there are one or two things on your list that really warrant stress. I will wager that most of the list is insignificant crap. We are wasting our creative energy on things that do not really matter and are completely out of our control. The next time you start to feel frustrated about a change, ask yourself, "Am I going to giggle about this in a week?"

How to play Know-it-All with your team:

1. Have everyone pair up. You can also have a trio. It is just easier with two people.

2. Each pair needs to work with another pair.

3. Decide who is going to start the sentence for each team.

4. Each person can only say one word at a time. The players alternate saying a word until they have a complete sentence. One team will start by asking a question one word at a time. The other pair will answer the question the same way. The team that just answered the question will then ask the other team a question (again one word at a time).

93

5. Try to say a word as fast as you can after your team member says their word. If you try to look for the right word or right answer, you will slow the game down, and it will lose momentum. You will never find the right word. Just say a word that follows the word that preceded it.

6. Do not just say random words. You must make sense.

7. Be sure to listen to your teammates.

8. The sentence will naturally come to an end. Once the team finishes answering the question, they should ask a question. Again, each person can only say one word at a time.

9. It is okay if you make a mistake. Laugh at the mistake and try again.

10. Remember to be open and flexible to your teammates and the words they choose. Be in the moment (listen). Prepare yourself because you do not know what word will come next. Embrace the change and be confident in your abilities. Have fun.

Chapter 11

Stay in the Game

Many of life's failures are people who did not realize how close they were to success when they gave up.

—Thomas Edison

A few years ago, I was shopping for office supplies and met Batman.

As I searched for file folders, I glanced down the aisle and saw Batman shopping with his mother. He was about five or six years old and wore the full Batman outfit. It was obvious that his mother was not pleased that Batman had accompanied her to the office supply store. She was frustrated. Certainly, her frustration was magnified not just because her child had dressed as Batman in public, but she was especially frustrated by the one small alteration he had made to the uniform. This Batman had chosen to wear his underwear over the costume, to appear truer to the original Caped Crusader. Because, as we all know, the original Batman wore briefs. And this Batman, being a creative risk taker, found a simple solution to his brief dilemma.

As I walked by Batman and his mother, I looked up without stopping and said, "Hi, Batman." I then continued my shopping.

Batman, astonished and excited that someone had acknowledged that he was indeed Batman, replied, "That's right. I'm Batman."

Batman then turned to his mother, "I'm Batman."

His mother was even more frustrated now that someone was encouraging her son's new occupation as Gotham City's crime fighter. She looked at me with disapproval and disappointment. She then said something to her son. In the distance, all I heard was the boy repeating, "I am Batman."

This story resonates with me. And not because secretly I would like to shop for office supplies dressed as Batman with my underwear on the outside of my outfit. I actually do, but the story resonates because the kid *believed* he was Batman. He didn't care what other people thought of his idea to dress as Batman and shop for office supplies. He was bold. He took a risk. He refused to listen to people who said he couldn't or shouldn't be Batman. I am sure his mother tried to persuade him not to wear the Batman outfit. And being a father myself, I understand the logic of small children. They do not give up. If they want something, *they stay in the game.*

And that is the secret. You see, Batman made me think about success in terms of improvisation. I thought about the most important message I ever learned from studying and performing improvisation: If you want to be successful, you have to *stay in the game.* If you quit, the game stops and you are guaranteed to fail.

Something might happen in the improv game that stops the momentum. A player might make a mistake. A player might say something that upsets the audience. No matter the action, you have to stay in the game to find success. The only action that leads to defeat in improvisation is quitting. Staying in the game means you will have to adjust, work harder, counter the action, work as a team, or just find a new path. Staying in the game is hard. It also leads to success.

Now, think about the concept of staying in the game at your work. I am not talking about quitting your job. I am talking about quitting goals and objectives, refusing to face a new challenge, or not taking a risk and trying something new. Quitting is easy. There is no work after giving up.

Staying in the game is hard. It is also fulfilling and rewarding. If something is easy, there is no fulfillment. When you put the time, energy, effort, and sweat into something, you are fulfilled. Staying in the game means you might need to learn something new, move out of your comfort zone, spend more time on the project, make a sacrifice, or increase your training.

Staying in the game means not giving up. The guarantee is that you will succeed. Success might not be tomorrow or even next week. It might not even be next month or next year. Staying in the game means success is still a possibility. If you quit, the guarantee is that you have failed.

When you decide to stay in the game, you cannot always worry about what other people think. How many times has someone questioned your ideas or process? How many times has someone stopped you from moving forward even though you knew you were right? Sometimes you have to be Batman. Think about the Wright brothers inventing the airplane. How many people thought they were crazy? What did they do? The Wright brothers told the crowd that they were Batman. Well, maybe one of them said they were Robin, but that doesn't matter. The point is that they stayed in the game and declared, "I am Batman."

To Be Successful, You Have to Stay in the Game

I have seen thousands of managers, executives, employees, and students play improvisation games with no experience and only a few seconds of instruction from me. They might not all have been creative or entertaining, but they met the objectives of the game. The successful volunteers made their share of mistakes. Sometimes they had to jump out of their comfort zone. They faced challenges. They had to work with a variety of teammates. Yet they all were successful.

Over the years, only a few people have failed playing an improvisation game with me. If you take away the volunteers who were overserved at the open bar, the ones who failed all have something in common: they quit during the game. They completely stopped the process of the game and just gave up. The audience and I still provided support. I would try to help them. The audience would help and voice encouragement. It didn't matter. In their minds, they failed before they started. Some would say, "I cannot play this game." Others would try to cover their quitting with an attitude that said, "Hey, I am going to half-ass this, but aren't I funny?" But they all quit. They quit in the middle. They quit at the end. They quit when the game became difficult. They quit because they refused to listen and learn something new.

Years ago, I presented a workshop to a small group of 20 or 25 managers. During a communication and teamwork exercise, a manager gave up during the game. She stopped trying. She had made up her mind before the game started that she was going to fail. I supported her during the game. I encouraged her. She reconsidered, engaged back into the game, and successfully finished. She was successful because she stayed in the game. Later, I spoke to her manager, who told me that how she played the game was how she worked. If a project became too difficult or involved learning or getting out of her comfort zone, she would quit, and someone else would finish the project.

I knew before she started the game that she would probably quit. I had spent several hours with her that day and had made my observations. It was obvious to me that her colleagues enabled her to quit. The difference is that I refused to allow her to quit during the improvisation game. I helped and supported her, but she had to do the work. And that is how I think she should be managed. She is completely capable. She just gets easily frustrated and disappointed in herself, and that leads to giving up. All of a sudden, quitting becomes a habit.

Quitting is the only action you really cannot do in an improvisation game. You can make mistakes. You can make poor choices. You can make choices that are not creative. As long as you stay in the game, you will have some form of success. You might not want the video of the improvisation game to appear on social media, but you will have met your objectives and finished the game.

Why Do We Look Up to Our Role Models? The Secret Is They Stayed in the Game

Sounds simple, huh? It is a message I have applied to my business, to how I perform, and even to my personal life. Most people can't stay in the game. They refuse to learn something new or work a little harder. Even more difficult is the decision to want to learn from their mistakes. We all know talented people who gave up on their dream when work or school became difficult or success didn't come soon enough. They had forgotten the most important principle of success: you have to stay in the game.

We quit things all the time. Sometimes we quit something small. Sometimes it is big. I think it is enlightening that the only action improvisation will not allow is the act of quitting. It is the only action that will cause you to fail. Every other action in improvisation allows you to continue to work toward your objective and to continue to create, learn, communicate, and succeed. The same principles that apply to improvisation apply to your job and your goals.

We all have role models. To some, our parents and grandparents are role models. Others look up to authors, inventors, colleagues, or historical figures. All of our role models have one thing in common: They all stayed in the game. They each had failures, obstacles, mistakes, and challenges. They are role models because they didn't quit. Research any historical figure and read his or her story. We never realize these famous or historical people had to deal with same types of failures, mistakes, or other obstacles until we watch their biographical movie.

As a side note, the preceding paragraph does not apply to heiresses, influencers, reality show contestants, and any "I did something stupid/strange/perverse/illegal and I made money/got away with it /posted it on the Internet" infamous people created by today's mass media. Sometimes, I have to clarify things for the kids.

I understand it is easy to talk about staying in the game. The tough part is to actually follow through. Maybe it is easier to examine and understand why people quit. From that information, we can try to avoid the common mistakes. Again, I want to go back to watching the thousands of people play the improvisation games during my presentations. Why did certain people have a hard time or give up? I think it comes down to two basic reasons.

People Quit Because They Are Afraid to Take a Risk or Try Something New

Some people fear the unknown. They refuse to take a risk because it involves something different. They fear they might not do well. They fear they will fail if they try to do something new. Guess what. They will fail. They will make mistakes. Everyone fails at some point when they first try something new. Most people learn from their mistakes and try again.

What if you had this same fear when you were a small child? At that time in your life, everything is new. You try to walk, you fall down, and you get up. You try to eat with a fork, you make a mess, and you stick the fork in your father's hair. We are all born with the ability to learn something new, fail, and then try again. As we grow older, we start to fear attempting something new because we are afraid of failing. We want perfection. We fear failure. Too many people go through life without taking a chance on their dream because they might fail. Who cares? Nobody is in the press box keeping statistics on your mistakes and failures. Nobody really cares.

People Quit Because They Are Afraid of What Other People Will Think

We really spend too much time caring about what other people might think of us. What if someone thinks that I am incapable? What if someone thinks I am foolish? In reality, the people who really matter don't care. We become inhibited when we worry too much about what a few people in the room think.

I was on the phone with a new client who was putting together a trade show and conference for her association. This was her first time putting together this conference, and she had some new ideas. A few of the board members were very negative about her new ideas. "They won't work," one said. "That's not how we usually do it," said another. My client had almost quit because of the negative people shooting down her ideas. She was too concerned about what the board members thought. I told my client that is how you know you are on the right track. Anytime someone says your new idea won't work just because it is different and new and "not what we have done before," you are on the right path. Guess what. My client stayed in the game and went forward with her ideas.[1]

Sometimes we all have to stand up and be Batman. We can't worry about making a mistake or even failing. We cannot worry about what other people will think. We just have to follow the examples of our role models and stay in the game. And if you need inspiration, go to the nearest office supply store and look down the aisle. There, someday, you will catch a glimpse of an adult in full Batman regalia, underwear on the outside, shopping for file folders. I am Batman.

Quick Ideas

The purpose of this exercise is to make you think about what you want to accomplish and what is stopping you. We tend to let very insignificant obstacles stand in the way of happiness. For example, maybe you want to start a business, but you are afraid you might fail and lose your investment.

Take a moment to write down your goals and dreams.

- If you could do anything, what would you do?

- What do you want to change at your job?

- Do you have any new ideas that relate to your job? How can you make those ideas a reality?

- What are your goals at your current job?

- Do you want to do something else?

- What new opportunities would you like to explore in your job and career?

- Do you have an idea to start a new business?

- Do you want to go back to school and start a new career?

Now think about what is really stopping you from moving forward.

- Are you just afraid you are going to fail?

- Are you worried about what your managers, colleagues, or friends might think?

Now think about the following questions:

• What would happen if your idea or plan failed?

• What would your customers, colleagues, managers, partners, vendors, or family do if your idea or plan failed?

Here's an example. When I left my job at the advertising agency to start my own business as a consultant, I knew there was always a possibility of failure. And I also knew that I might lose some money, end up broke, and have to eat buttered pasta every night for dinner. If I failed, then I would go find another job. I was willing to accept the risk.

Take control of your goals. To find happiness, you have to take a risk. You have to stay in the game. Remember, you are Batman.

Chapter 12

Learn to Communicate in the Moment

*The problem with communication . . . is the illusion that it has
been accomplished.*

—George Bernard Shaw

I do not think I can handle another video conference call. I cannot
handle anything to do with the entire process. I cannot handle
the 32 emails to set up the call. I cannot handle connecting to the
conference number and then waiting forever for the host to start the
call or "to be allowed" into the call. I cannot handle trying to hear
the one person in the room who is speaking 16 ft. from the speaker.
I cannot handle that the actual call takes four times longer than if
I just spoke to one person.

I cannot handle looking at someone's ceiling fan for 40 minutes.
I cannot handle Kyle deciding to sit in front of a window that faces
the sun. I cannot handle Lisa not knowing she is on mute.

I cannot handle that some managers and employees collect conference calls on their calendar like hunting trophies on a wall: "Man,
I am swamped today. My plate is completely full because I have so
many irons in the fire. I cannot meet for lunch/Pilates/hot yoga/
coffee/a smoothie bowl today because I have four Zoom calls."

I do love when your dog barks and you go close the door. And then your dog keeps barking. I love when someone walks into frame behind you, looks around, and then quickly walks away. I love looking at your bookshelf for clues about your personal life.

Maybe I am obsessing. The video conference call is just a symptom of a larger communication problem. My favorite part of the call is when everyone agrees with a comment, using a special conference call language. Everyone immediately says the same thing using some hybrid language involving business-school babble, current executive-speak, and corporate-meeting catchphrases. Does the following call sound familiar?

> *"Our world-class marketing team synergizes our global brand influence with a tiered multilevel approach to scalability," said the super important manager, mimicking the big words a vice president said at a recent conference.*
>
> *"I agree. Our core competency is embedded in our ability to transition our resources into processes that move our brand forward with critical value-adds," said the person on the call that has not said anything until this moment, not really understanding any of the conversation.*
>
> *"Yes, let me tee up something here. The truth of the matter is making sure our deliverables leverage our people as resources that will optimize best-in-class standards for our stakeholders," said the manager who just repeats something someone else said so they can hear themselves speak.*

I hit the mute button or turn off my camera before I choke on my granola bar. I cannot handle that the more people on the call, the less actual work will be achieved.

And, finally, I cannot handle the scheduling of the conference call. Space missions are shorter than the time it takes to schedule the average conference call. Let me break down the scheduling of a typical call. I must warn everyone, this is graphic in nature and for mature audiences only:

1. You email me about a possible conference call.[1]

2. I email some available dates.

3. You email back that the vice president of Global Brand Management needs to attend the call, but she has a meeting in Singapore.

4. I email back with some more available dates.

5. You select a date. It is not one of the available dates that I had previously emailed you. Instead, you select a date from the phantom calendar that exists only to please you and the vice president of Global Brand Management. Also, my son has a baseball game on the date you selected.

6. You email me. I email you. Someone else joins the email party in an attempt to select a date. At this point, the amount of emails generated to schedule this conference call is exactly the same as the number of spam emails I receive in a week offering me discounted pharmaceuticals, an excellent cannot-miss stock opportunity from an Eastern European company, and a magical hair loss treatment.

7. During the time we have attempted to schedule a conference call, which in no way should classify as effective or productive communication, the Earth has made four complete rotations, salmon have spawned, movie stars have married and divorced, political fortunes were won and lost; and a group of Sherpas and several future motivational speakers have reached the summit of Mount Everest.

8. We finally schedule the call.

9. The Earth makes several more rotations. The Sherpas guide their party back to base camp.

Learn to Communicate in the Moment

10. The vice president of Global Brand Management has scheduled a meeting during the conference call. You email me about trying to change the date. I return your email with other possible dates. You send me an alternate date that is also the same afternoon of my son's baseball game.

11. We agree on a time and date. We have the conference call at the appointed time. The vice president of Global Brand Management can join the conference call when her meeting in Singapore falls through due to an international incident. However, they can only call in from an airport lounge, so it is hard to hear her.

12. The vice president of Global Brand Management does not speak during the call.

13. The conference call ends. At the end of the call, someone says, "When do you want to schedule another call?" I do a spit take and choke on my granola bar.

14. The Sherpas drink tea and laugh because they do not have to deal with conference calls.[2]

The Conference Call Is Just One Bad Communication Habit—There Are Many Others

When did we think it would be more effective for eight people to spend an hour babbling when only two of the people on the call need to talk?

The conference call is just one of many bad communication habits we have picked up over the years. We learn from our surroundings. We grow up in a world of conference calls and convoluted emails and business speak that offers big words but few actual details, and we think we are effectively communicating. We are not.

But we can change. We can learn. We can break the chain. If we just focus on a few simple areas, we can become better communicators.

Here are the key communication choices improvisation has taught me and that I have learned by watching thousands of audience volunteers play the games:

1. Deliver the right number of details at the right time.

2. Be present and in the moment during communication.

3. Define constant communication.

4. Create communication that makes your recipient feel comfortable, confident, and in control.

5. Create a partnership in your communication.

6. Be patient and set the right tone.

Deliver Detailed Communication

Everybody thinks they are communicating with solid details. We are usually giving either too much or too little information.

Go around the office and ask each person to stand. And then tell them to take a step-up. Each person will step up differently because there is no common definition for step-up. This is guaranteed, much like if a reality show celebrity makes a movie, it will have the charisma, energy, and soul of an egg salad sandwich. I sometimes use a trust/communication game where one person closes their eyes and relies on another person (their eyes open) to communicate to them how to navigate the room. I remember one time an executive saw an electrical cord across the floor and told his partner (with the closed eyes) to step up to avoid an obstacle. The executive with his eyes closed raised his foot about three feet high and made such a huge step up that he could have easily cleared a small pony.

We have to give definitive details. The more detail we give, the more comfortable, confident, and in control our recipient will be with the communication. The executive playing the trust game should have said, "We want to avoid an electrical cord, so lift one foot up six inches and then six inches forward." Isn't that a more detailed, effective communication?

The key is to give the right amount of detail. If you give too many details to someone who does not need them, the recipient tunes out. They are overwhelmed and cannot decide. If you give too few details, the recipient might make a mistake. Some people who want an abundance of detail are unable to decide when they do not have all the information.

We tend to give the same amount of detail to everyone. We each receive information differently. If we communicate the same to everyone and we all receive information differently, then there is going to be one big, fat disconnection.

How do you know how much detail your communication recipient needs? Well, you could read the next section of this chapter. The paragraph directly following this paragraph will have the answer. See, wasn't that a detailed answer?

Communicate in the Moment and Define Constant Communication

Improvisation is about working in the moment. When you are performing without a script or rehearsal, your whole presence and mind must work in the moment. If you start thinking about the last game, the next game, or whether the original *Road House* movie is better than the new *Road House* movie (it is) you will fail.[3] It is impossible to achieve success in improvisation if you do not live in the moment. Again, improvisation forces you to make the right choice.

Are you in the moment in your job? When you are on the phone, are you also going through your email? When you communicate, are you listening to the other person or just waiting for your turn to speak? When you are on a conference call, do you start daydreaming about renting an RV and taking a road trip to Key West?

We try to do too much at one time and cover ourselves by calling it multitasking. Folding the laundry and watching the new hit show on Netflix is a great way to multitask. Speaking with your client and checking your email at the same time is not such a good multitask. You are missing details. You are missing tone, inflection, and other clues that will help you make the right communication decision. When *you* are the customer, you expect *your* vendors to communicate and work in the moment.

If we stay in the moment, we will quickly understand how much and what kind of detailed information to provide. We will pick up the clues that will help us make better communication decisions. When I perform and ask for volunteers to come on stage, I am watching them from the moment they leave their seats. The more information I have, the easier it is to make the right choice in my communication. How fast they came to the stage, the strength of their voice, are they breathing heavily, how they introduce themselves are all clues. I watch their eyes and body language. I may have noticed the volunteer before the event or overheard something they said. This information is immediately processed so that I can give the volunteer the right details for them to achieve success. If I am not in the moment, I am just guessing. And I will usually guess wrong.

By working in the moment, we understand that we cannot communicate the same way to each person. For example, some of my clients are chit-chat clients. Some of my clients are very down to business. Have you ever seen a down-to-business person and a chit-chat person work together? Find a wall. Make a fist. Now, hit

Learn to Communicate in the Moment

your fist against the wall several times. It is pretty much the same thing.

If you chit-chat with a down-to-business person, they think you are wasting their time. If you do not chit-chat to a chit-chat person, they think you do not care or do not like them. Communicate in the moment and you will understand who you are communicating to in every situation.

Let us say I am working on a project with Bob in accounting. Bob is very organized. Bob is a planner. Bob is down to business. Bob wants to speak every day to me about the project we are working on together. What do I think about Bob? I think Bob is a maniacal micromanager who does not trust me.

Now, let us talk about me. I want to talk once a week about the project. Bob tells his friend Susan in accounting that I am irresponsible. He says I spend too much time goofing around and making jokes. He thinks I am not making the project a priority.

Bob and I are both wrong. Bob and I are so focused on building a wall between us that we have a hard time working together. Bob and I work differently. We communicate differently. If neither one of us is in the moment, we will never realize our potential. I think Bob and I could work as a very effective and productive team. My creativity and Bob's organizational skills would complement each other and produce results.

What is the solution? Bob is the smart one. Bob calls me and says we should meet twice a week. I tell Bob that is a great idea. **Now, we have defined what constant communication means to both of us.** We are both in the moment and have started building a foundation. Bob and I are going to make a great team. We have defined expectations.

Bob wants to meet at 8 a.m. I tell Bob not to push it and that 10 a.m. will be just fine. Remember, Bob, we work differently.

Make Your Recipient Feel Comfortable, Confident, and in Control

I think all decisions are based on communicating the answers to three questions:

1. Am I making the recipient of my communication feel comfortable?

2. Am I making the recipient feel confident?

3. Am I making the recipient feel in control?

Think about the last time you made a large or small purchase—a car, a house, a cell phone, even a tube of toothpaste. Why did you choose the car you purchased over the other cars? Did you feel comfortable? Did you feel confident in your decision? Did you feel in control? I would wager the answer is yes.

How did you become comfortable, confident, and in control? I am sure brand and advertising played a role. Word of mouth from friends and family contributed. You probably did your own research. Finally, the salesperson played a part. Once you decided that you were comfortable, confident, and in control of your decision, you made a choice. If you did not, you would not have made the purchase.

A few years ago, we had a huge hail storm where I live. The entire neighborhood had to buy new roofs. I had never purchased a roof. I know one thing about roofs: they are above the house and are designed to keep water out. That is the extent of my roof knowledge.

I spoke with three roofing contractors. The prices for all three were comparable. Which contractor would do the best job? Only one made me feel comfortable, confident, and in control. He gave me a packet of information. He gave me his insurance information. He gave me references. He told me exactly when the job would be done, what materials would be used, and how the workers cleaned up the job site. I chose my contractor because he made me feel comfortable, confident, and in control. The contractor gave me the right amount of detail. He was accessible and answered my questions. His tone was positive and patient.

As you communicate, ask the three questions. Figure out what your recipient needs to be comfortable, confident, and in control. Are you giving the right details at the right time? Are you being patient, understanding, and positive? Understand how *you* respond as a customer, and you will become a more powerful communicator.

Make Your Communication 50/50

During most of my presentations, I play an improvisation game that focuses on communication. I talk about how 50% of my job is to give detailed information to the recipient. And 50% of the recipient's job is to listen, focus, and be involved. I have probably used this term 1,000 times. Nobody has ever asked what the other 50% for each person entails. Everybody just shakes their head and thinks to themselves, "Yeah, 50 plus 50 is 100, so I guess everything adds up."

And now here is the answer. Each party has 50% of the responsibility to give detailed information and 50% of the responsibility to listen and be involved. Math is really not that important when you are trying to make a point.

The point is to encourage involvement by both parties in the communication. During the improvisation exercise, I am trying to communicate a location, occupation, and object to my volunteer. Sometimes the participant is involved and part of the process. And sometimes they stand on the side of the stage, inching farther and farther away from the action. When it comes time to guess the location, occupation, and object, who do you think does better? Of course, the participant who is involved in the process is more successful.

There is one industry that speaks to their customers at 100% to 0%: spam email. Spam senders do not care what the recipient wants, needs, or understands. Spammers just keep "communicating" one way until something hits. And how do we respond to spam? We hit the delete key. Do you speak to your colleagues, clients, partners, and vendors at 100% to 0%, not expecting any involvement or anything in return? Or do you speak to them more on a 50/50 basis?

At one time or another, someone has treated us like spam. We are deleted and ignored. If we give the right information and create a partnership in our communication, we will not be treated like spam. Otherwise, I will give you the same amount of attention that I give to the 162 spam emails I receive each day about "can't miss" stocks and Viagra.

We All Want Positive and Patient Communication

I have discussed how important creating a positive environment is to our work. Think about communication as a fork in the road. You can take the left way and be impatient, frustrated, and negative in your communication. Or you can go the right way and be patient and positive. Your communication goal remains the same. You just choose a more positive path to get there, a path that will include less stress and fewer visits to the doctor for high blood pressure and heart attacks.

Communication is vital to success in improvisation. I view improvisation as a microcosm of successful teamwork. The basic aspects that make performers successful are the same tenets that will make you successful. Like anything, we learned most of these skills when we were children. Along the way, we just have to be reminded of them. We all have the ability to communicate more successfully. We get lazy. We start bad habits. We become frustrated. We can change, though. If you just focus on a few of the ideas I have mentioned, you will become a stronger communicator.

I have to go now. I have a Zoom call, followed by a Teams call, followed by Google Meet, followed by a regular conference call. I hope to see at least one ceiling fan and hear one dog barking.

Quick Ideas

Here are a few reminders to help you communicate effectively.

- Put a note near your computer that says, "Step up" or "Stay in the moment." This will remind you to listen and provide the right details.

- Pay attention to how you communicate to your colleagues, customers, partners, and vendors.

- Are you in the moment?

- Are you listening?

- Are you focusing on the conversation?

These small reminders will make a huge difference. Just a few words taped to your computer or portfolio will remind you to work toward more detailed, positive, and successful communication.

I also want to emphasize again something very important in this chapter. We make decisions based on feeling comfortable, confident, and in control. Every point in this chapter (and book) can help you reach those three goals in your communication.

As a review, think about the following in helping your recipient feel comfortable, confident, and in control:

- How much detail does the recipient need?

- Have I given the right details at the right time?

Make the Right Choice

- What does constant communication mean to the recipient?

- How can I be more positive and patient in my communication?

- Have I involved the recipient in the communication? What can I do to create more involvement?

Understanding why people make decisions will help you communicate more effectively. Figure out what does and does not work for you. As long as you take responsibility, you will make the right choice.

Chapter 13

Communication Intervention

First learn the meaning of what you say, and then speak.
—Epictetus

When people talk, listen completely. Most people never listen.
—Ernest Hemingway

Public speaking is the art of diluting a two-minute idea with a two-hour vocabulary.
—John Fitzgerald Kennedy

I *need to tee up a very important issue. I know you have a full plate, but I wanted to straw-man a paradigm shift in our strategy. The purpose is to create a clearer vision by doing a process check on our overall goals. The deliverables would produce more bandwidth and connect the dots within our cross-functional organization.*

If you have any idea what the first paragraph means, then you need to sit down, slowly put away your phone, and take a deep breath. This is an intervention. I am here to help you. You are addicted to empty business phrases that have become overused, overhyped, and overwrought.[1]

We are a society of mimics. We hear a word or phrase, and it becomes part of our business vocabulary. The words really don't mean anything, yet we use them. We speak them. We email them. We create PowerPoint slides and put them in circles or upside-down triangles.

If we use these words, employees and customers will know what we are talking about. People will listen to us, right? Or their eyes could glaze over as they stare into the back of your skull while daydreaming about their next trip to Costco to buy patio furniture pillows, smoked salmon, a three-month supply of paper towels, and one hell of a tiramisu.

Each conference I attend, I listen to presentations from the vice president, executive director, CEO, someone from HR, the head of accounting, and the person in charge of the new project. Power-Point slides cascade off the screen with upside-down triangles and interlocking circles. Each slide is packed with too many words, too small print, and are chock-full of business speak. The audience is bored. We stab our leg with the free pen that lights up to prevent a cliché-induced sleep. We have no idea what it really means to have a paradigm shift, but it sounds painful and sudden.

And if we are talking like this at our conferences and meetings, then we are probably at our jobs speaking to our customers, employees, colleagues, partners, and vendors the same way. We must speak more clearly. We must try to connect with each of them as individuals or as small groups, doing our best to customize the message. We must stop communicating the same way to every person. Do you think all of your customers and employees will respond to the same message?

Try this experiment. Call your spouse and say, *"I need to touch base with you about tonight's deliverables. There is nothing in the pipeline, and our direct reports expressed interest for an all-hands, off-site meeting. Our stakeholders would like to leverage their best-in-class quantitative tools to create synergy and ask for a risk assessment for a future incentive trip."*

Translation: "What are we doing tonight for dinner? There is nothing at home to eat and the kids want to go to Chipotle. Isabella and Zander received good grades this semester and are begging for a trip to Colorado."

We don't use business speak with our spouses or our friends because we care. We care about what they think and how they react. We care about them understanding our thoughts and ideas. Shouldn't we care the same about our employees and customers? You can talk about leverage, connectivity, linkage grids, and core competencies only so many times before the words stop having meaning—if they ever had any real purpose or meaning. What does "synergistic customer alignment" mean to you? Does your customer understand or care?

Improvisation Just Might Show Us the Way

Many of the improvisation games I use involve communication among participants. In a previous chapter, I discussed the big-picture communication skills that are needed to be successful. Now, I want to focus on the little things that allow us to work and communicate more effectively, productively, and successfully.

1. *Listen.* I know I have mentioned listening in other chapters. Still, it is the foundation of all communication. Do you know what happens when my audience volunteers listen? They become more creative and productive. More importantly, they play the game with more confidence and have more fun.

   All communication starts when we actively listen. We can all be better listeners. We just have to make the right choices to become a better listener. If we are speaking to someone in person, make eye contact. If we are on the phone, *stop going through your email and listen.*[2]

I do not have the secret to becoming a better listener. I could write 2,000 words about listening, but it really just comes down to this: *take responsibility and listen.*[3]

An audience member asked this question recently, "I am not very good with names. Do you have any tips?" I have received this question many times. My answer is always the same. Do you know your name? Do you know the names of your children, parents, and other family members? Do you know the names of your friends? Of course you do. So you really do not have a problem with names. You have a problem listening when you meet someone new and they say their name.

Improvisation forces the performers to listen, be more present, and be in the moment. Often after an exercise, I ask the audience volunteers what they were thinking about while they were on stage. They answer: the objective, the game, or the team. Improvisation forces the audience member to focus on what is important and *be present*. We are at our best when we are present and in the moment. We are better leaders, communicators, innovators, and teammates. And it all starts with listening.

2. *Speak clearly and directly.* Just because the vice president standing on stage at the conference uses "leverage," "bandwidth," and "slide deck" in the same sentence does not mean we all have to speak that way. If you wouldn't talk to your sweet Aunt Joyce that way, then you shouldn't speak to your customers and employees that way.

I was at a recent client meeting where they described their objectives for the year. One of the goals was client centricity.

I am still waiting for the explanation, definition, or purpose of client centricity. I guess it means that the company is focused on the client. First, I am pretty sure every business is focused on the client. Second, I really wonder about the first meeting when someone brought up client centricity as an objective or goal. Did everyone at the meeting immediately agree this was the best term? How many had to look up the word? I am not even sure it is a real word. "Yep, client centricity is perfect. I have no idea what it means, but it perfectly describes our purpose. It sounds like we are centered on the client and that produces electricity between us and them. Yeah, it's electric. I love it. Let's run with it."

During one improvisation game, the players have to communicate a location, occupation, and an object. They cannot speak English; they can speak only a language called Gibberish. It is amazing how easy it is to think you are communicating in perfect detail, only to find that the recipient doesn't have a clue. During one game, a gentleman attempted to communicate a giraffe to his teammate. The recipient thought she understood correctly and signaled that she understood. Seconds later, the woman was rolling on the floor. When asked what she was communicating by rolling on the floor, the woman, without hesitation said, "I was an egg roll." To this day, I have no idea how a giraffe became an egg roll. I do know someone was not speaking clearly or directly. Or someone else was very hungry.

3. *Slow down*. Sometimes participants are so quick to communicate a message that they rush. They fly through the details, leaving some very important points out of the message. Worse, I have seen players in a hurry start in the middle rather than at the beginning. The result is poor communication. When I remind the audience volunteers to slow down or

Communication Intervention

to start from the beginning, they immediately become more successful in communicating the message. Let me give you a quick example of some audience volunteers rushing (yes, this is a true story):

- I communicate "porcupine" to audience member #1. I act out a porcupine. I show that something hurts when I touch the porcupine. I am hitting all the details of porcupine.

- Audience member #1 rushes through the message as he communicates porcupine to audience member #2.

- Audience member #2, thinking he is correct, now thinks "porcupine" is a "rabbit."

- Mr. Rabbit (audience member #2) communicates to audience member #3. Again, he rushes.

- When it comes time to guess, audience member #3 guesses, "Snake?"

- Mr. Rabbit then yells out, "In my pocket? Why would I put a snake in my pocket!"

- I then ask Mr. Rabbit for his guess. Mr. Rabbit says, "Rabbit."

- I say, "In your pocket? Why would you put a rabbit in your pocket?"

The audience member rushed through the communication. They forgot details or communicated the details too fast. Yes, the audience laughed and enjoyed watching the process and communication failure. My point was easily made to slow down, focus on the details, take your time, and be patient during communication. Also, sometimes porcupines are fun to imitate.

4. *Yes, you can start over. Yes, you can try a different tack.* Watching audience members communicate the messages in

the improvisation game is a great way to see how we communicate at our jobs. Sometimes, by watching others play the game, we can discover a more successful way.

The reality is that sometimes our communication doesn't work. Rather than pound the square peg into the round hole, why don't we find another way? Again, when the audience members stop, regroup, and try a different tack, they are able to communicate the messages and achieve the objectives.

Have you ever seen someone communicate "giraffe" without speaking? I stood on a chair. I pointed to my neck and made a gesture that indicated length. I stuck out my tongue. My partner didn't understand. The audience was rolling with laughter. I stopped, regrouped, added more details and tried something different. I imitated an elephant. Then I imitated a giraffe. Boom. My partner understood and I was successful.

5. *Let the person finish*. A common mistake is speaking too soon. The communicator starts delivering the message, and before he is finished the recipient says, "Okay, I got it." And that's when the trouble starts. Every single time, the recipient's impatience results in miscommunication. Be patient. Receive the entire communication before making a decision.

6. *Work together to focus and deliver a common message*. During one of my communication games, two players work together to deliver a message to another player. When they are at their best, the two players are working in concert to deliver the message. When there is trouble, one player is acting out their interpretation of an egg roll while the other is imitating a giraffe. The recipient's head is moving side to side fast enough to cause a breeze. Work together and focus.

7. *Be patient*. After watching thousands of audience members play these games, I have learned quite a bit about what makes

125

Communication Intervention

us successful communicators. One of the very simple yet remarkable discoveries has to do with attitude. I am pretty sure I have never had an audience member act impatient or frustrated during a communication exercise. Participants might not get the message correct. They might not understand what the other player is communicating. It doesn't matter. When the audience members stay patient, they eventually find a way to achieve success.

What happens when we do not understand? We get frustrated. We get impatient. But communication is a circle. You are at the top and I am at the bottom. We can go the left way and be impatient and frustrated. Or we can go the right way and be positive and understanding. Both routes are the same distance. One is a better trip.

Finally, the next time someone uses business speak, just giggle. When you really think about it, these words are so absurd that the only true reaction is to giggle. After a few giggles, the vice president probably will stop interfacing with the direct reports and start speaking clearly to the team.

Quick Ideas

Okay, this communication intervention is almost over. Here are just a few final thoughts. My goal is to change society one person at a time.

1. *Avoid using acronyms with customers.* We have enough acronyms in our lives.

2. *Ask questions and become involved.* If someone tells you the organization is going through a paradigm shift, ask what that *really* means. What specifically is going to happen? How does

---

it affect me, and what is my role? When will this shift take place, and will it affect the midnight shift or my power shift transmission? Speak up and refuse to accept business speak as an answer.

3. *Be patient.* Yes, I know I have said this before. I am going to say it again. In the future, we will always understand everything everyone says because we will have small microchips implanted in our brains. Until then, you may have to repeat yourself.

4. *Be positive.* People get frustrated. People get stressed. People have heart attacks. Stay positive and you can avoid the first three.

Here is a fun game to try with the team. This is a four-person game:

1. Explain that you (the starter) are going to get a location, occupation, and an animal from the team.

2. The three other volunteers are going to go outside the room where they cannot hear. Ask the team for the suggestions.

3. Ask the first person to come into the room (the other two stay outside the room where they cannot hear). Communicate the three messages (location, occupation, animal) without speaking. Act out the messages and paint a picture. You can make sound effects; you just can't speak. Ask volunteer #1 if they understand (but you don't want them to guess).

4. Volunteer #2 then comes into the room. Volunteer #1 communicates the same three messages. They can do exactly what the first volunteer did, add more details, or do something different to communicate the messages. Hopefully, they are right. We just want to make sure they at least have a guess.

5. Volunteer #3 comes into the room. Volunteer #2 communicates the three messages to volunteer #3.

6. Then we see if #3 can guess all three. If they can't, then ask #2. If #2 does not get it right, ask #1.

7. Ask each volunteer what they learned. What did they do that was successful? What did they do that didn't work? How can they apply what they learned in this communication game to their job?

Make the Right Choice

Chapter 14

The Creative Mind: Thinking without a Script

The best way to have a good idea is to have lots of ideas.

—Linus Pauling

The middle-aged man in the front row was a creative zombie. He appeared normal at first. He laughed. He participated. That's how zombies fool us non-zombie people. Zombie people deviously trick us to aid in their deception. Now, do not get me wrong. He wasn't a walking-dead, flesh-eating zombie who stalks the streets with his arms outstretched, grunting. No, he was a creative zombie— a working-dead, idea-eating zombie who stalks the hallways and cubicles with his hands in the air, grunting. They walk among us. Somehow, other creative zombies had killed his creative passion and spirit. If you listen closely, you can always spot a creative zombie. When they grunt, they say things such as, "This is the way we have always done it."

At first, I did not realize the man was a creative zombie. I had just finished explaining the next exercise when he said something so scary, I jumped back in horror. I knew right then he was a zombie. We were about to play a simple creativity game. The game starts with a word. For this exercise, I chose an animal. The person sitting next to me then has to take the last letter of my animal and come up with a different animal that starts with that letter. The next person follows suit until everyone in the room has participated. There is only one rule: You cannot repeat animals. The objective of the game is for each person in the room to say a different animal.[1]

It's an easy game. If you are stuck, audience members can help by yelling out an animal. I have played this game hundreds of times.

The zombie in the front looked confused. He said something to the person sitting next to him. He shook his head. He folded his arms and let out a frustrated sigh. The game was about to start. "I think there is a problem," he said.

"This game will not work," he said. "There is only one animal that starts with the letter Z."

I shuddered. I stepped back in horror. He was a zombie. He could turn everyone in the room into creative zombies. I had to stop him before he turned the others.

So many responses to the zombie swirled in my head:

1. *How many animals are there that end in the letter Z?*

2. *Why are you so concerned that someone will say an animal that ends in Z, perplexing and confusing you?*

3. *How do you know you will need a Z animal when it is your turn?*

4. *Really, are you sure there is only one animal?*

5. *Do you need to eat a cookie, because I do not think your brain has enough glucose to sustain reasonable thought?*

This is what society does to our creative spirit. Society rolls it up into a ball, lights it on fire, and then runs over it with a 4×4 truck with tires the size of a water buffalo. We are so beaten down that we give up. We no longer see possibilities. We create rules where rules do not exist. We see only obstacles. Go talk to your child about creativity. Children do not have creative obstacles. I remember my three-year-old daughter telling me she was the abominable snow-man.[2] She did not stop and think, "Hey I am not a seven-foot-tall creature covered in white fur that appears in Himalayan folk tales and in the story of Rudolph the Red-Nosed Reindeer." Instead, she was a three-foot-high ball of energy running around the house in a pink tutu and telling everyone that she was, in fact, the abominable snowman.

I do not have any talismans to protect you from creative zom-bies. Again, it comes down to choices. We each have to make the choices that will put us in a better position to create. We can make the choices that generate energy and fuel for our creative spirit. And even if we make those choices, we still have a difficult road in communicating our ideas, selling our ideas, and implementing our ideas. Creative zombies lurk everywhere. If you are ever stranded on a deserted island, just come up with an idea. A creative zombie will show up in a few moments to tell you one of the following:

- Your idea will not work.
- Your idea is ridiculous.
- Your idea lives with the fishes.

Creativity is just a fancy word for problem solving. We all have the ability to solve problems and we all have the ability to create. As we go through life, we start making small choices that hinder our creativity. We lose the ability to ponder the possibilities. Instead, we see only the obstacles. If we focus too much on why we cannot do something, we will never take any risks.

I confront creative zombies all the time. They have no faith. They do not believe their colleagues are creative. I can undeniably say that *everyone* has the ability to create. Every time I speak, I am amazed by the creative abilities of my audience and their eagerness to step outside their comfort zone. I have heard too many times from creative zombies that "my group of accountants/bankers/engineers/IT technicians/salespeople/fill in the blank are not creative." I have proven this statement wrong each time.

Improvisation unlocks a participant's creativity. We are encouraged and supported. During each keynote, I am surprised by at least one magical moment. Why do the improvisation games unleash the participant's creativity?

1. Participants are free to make a mistake. There is no script, no plan, and no rehearsal. The freedom encourages taking risks.

2. The positive support from the audience encourages their creativity.

3. Nobody is critiquing their idea. In improvisation there is no right or wrong choice. Some choices are better than others. And we are always trying to make the right choice.

4. During the improvisation game, each person's contribution is valued.

5. Each participant is an equal.

During a recent pre-event Zoom call, the client asked questions about the different activities I do with the audience. I explained an exercise I do at the beginning of my keynote called "Bunny, Bunny, Bunny." I ask everyone to put their thumbs on their temples, make bunny ears with their hands, turn to the person next to them, and say, "Bunny, Bunny, Bunny." Is it silly? Yep. Is it out of some people's comfort zone? Yep.[3]

The "Bunny, Bunny, Bunny" exercise is about taking a risk. I want the audience to jump out of their comfort zone. Yes, I want

Make the Right Choice

them to smile and laugh at the silliness, creating energy in the room. I also want them to realize that if we (the audience) face a risk together, it is not as difficult. By participating, each audience member supports the others. The energy of the entire audience supporting each other is powerful. Nobody is saying, "You look like an idiot with your bunny ears."

Some in the audience will immediately make bunny ears. Some will tentatively look around, realize everyone is making bunny ears, and then join the activity. It is simple and awesome.

Back to the Zoom call. After describing the bunny ears activity almost exactly as I have done in the previous paragraphs, the client stared into the camera perplexed. He offered that this exercise is not right for this group of financial and insurance professionals. "I do not think they will do it," he said. "It might be too silly." Other people on the call agreed. I had to explain that this is event number 2,505 for me and the bunny ears exercise works with every group.

I wish someone had recorded me "selling" the bunny ears exercise. Sometimes, I take a step back in wonder and realize this is my job. I am talking about bunny ears with financial executives. Finally, the client relented and trusted my experience.

Did the bunny ears work? Yep, they always do. Was it silly? Yep, that is the whole point. The coolest part is the attendees represented 25+ different countries. Some in the audience received my presentation through translators. It was probably one of the most awesome "Bunny, Bunny, Bunny" experiences of my career. The moment truly inspired me. If I can get attendees from 25 countries to make bunny ears at their colleagues, there is hope for this world.

It easy to fear the unknown. Innovation is getting out of our comfort zone and trying something new. The bunny ears exercise was new to this client. He feared the unknown.

We must stand up and fight the creative zombies. Rally around each other and do not allow the creative zombies to turn you. As you march to defend the creative universe, here are some choices that will help you achieve success.

Do Not Analyze and Create at the Same Time

As soon as we start analyzing an idea, we have stopped the creative process. During a creative session, someone presents an idea. Our first reaction is to analyze the idea: Will it work? Do we have the budget? Is the idea feasible? We have stopped generating ideas because our minds cannot create and analyze at the same time. Innovation wants energy. It wants to build off other ideas. If we stop, we lose the energy and momentum. This is the reason why improvisation does not allow you to say no during a scene. As soon as someone rejects the idea, the creativity stops because it has nowhere to go.

When I am performing an improvisation exercise with audience volunteers, their creative energy explodes. Each idea builds on another idea. Why? The performers never stop to analyze their idea. Each volunteer continues to create with no fear or hesitation. The audience responds with positive support. And the performer generates more ideas.

Try this: split the creative session into two sections. The first section of time is for creating ideas. Reject your initial reaction to analyze. Instead, build on each other's ideas. Support each idea with encouragement. Use the energy in the room to create more ideas. During the second section, analyze the ideas.

Remember, creativity is not a race to come up with the first idea. Build on each other's ideas during the creative process. Use the energy created during the process. If we stop to analyze, we cannot build on each idea. We have one idea. And after we dissect, question, ponder, dispute, and mutilate the idea, we probably will not feel like producing any more ideas.

Create. Analyze. Just do not try and do both at the same time.

Expand Your Possibilities

Remember the Last Letter of the Animal's Name game? When I play this game with my groups, I tell them that there is only one rule: you cannot reuse animal names. Once someone uses an animal for a letter, it is off the board. What happens? Participants create their own rules. Here are just a few of the rules participants have made up while playing this game:[4]

- We cannot use dinosaurs.
- Unicorns do not exist. We cannot use fairy-tale animals.
- We cannot use insects.
- Spiders are not animals.
- We cannot make up animals.
- We cannot use marine life because they are not animals.
- You cannot use the Easter Bunny because it does not exist.

The creative zombies are so quick to pull out their imaginary rule book and cite rules that do not exist. "Section five, paragraph six, says we cannot, under any circumstances, use unicorns, centaurs, orcs, goblins, gremlins, hellhounds, pixies, satyrs, or any other animal that has appeared in a fairy tale, nursery rhyme, or animated Disney movie."

The only rule I give participants is that they cannot reuse animal names. I never said you could not make up animals (a dee-dee, a zebu). I did not say you could not put an adjective in front of the word (a nefarious tiger, a neighborly owl, a nasty giraffe). I did not say you could not use unicorns. The purpose of the game is to demonstrate how quickly we shrink our possibility box. When we shrink our possibility box, we run out of ideas. We struggle. I want to see how the group reacts when we eliminate animals. After we shrink our possibility box, we look for an idea and only then notice the box is practically empty. Maybe there is one used-up idea rolling around the bottom. If you stop making rules where rules do not exist, you can expand your possibility box.

Sure, there will be lots of ideas that may not work. There will also be lots of ideas that may work.

Relax

When I play the Last Letter of the Animal's Name game, I want the participants to struggle. As I said in the preceding section, I want to force them to expand their possibility box. Sometimes, participants become so frustrated they freeze. They cannot come up with an animal for their letter, and they do not know how to expand their possibility box. They start to feel tense. Their creative mind stops working. I always ask why they were not able to come up with an animal. The answer is always the same, "Too much pressure."

These are smart people. If I gave them five minutes, I am sure they could write down 100 animal names. Why did they struggle? Why did they feel pressure? Do they think in their next review someone might say, "Well, we would like to promote you, but you were unable to come up with an animal that started with the letter P, so we are going to have to put you on probation."

Guess what happens. Every person that struggled to come up with an animal when it was their turn was able to come up with an animal when it wasn't their turn. Why? When it wasn't their turn, there was no pressure. Their mind was relaxed. They did not care if they came up with an animal or not.

Think about when you are most creative. Some of the answers I have heard from audiences are exercising, gardening, sleeping, showering, cooking, and spending time with their children. All of these answers have something in common: relaxation.

Is there a place that fuels your creativity? Is there a time of day when you are more creative? Creativity needs energy for fuel. And sometimes that energy and fuel is taking a deep breath and relaxing.

Reward the Time Spent Creating the Idea

Let us be realistic. Most ideas do not see the light of day. Ideas are analyzed, dissected, ignored, critiqued, and finally dismissed. What happens when an employee's ideas are always slapped down? Eventually, the employee stops coming up with ideas. We take rejection personally. We have a hard time separating our ideas from our personal feelings. "They never use my ideas," the employee says after getting rejected. "There is no point in giving ideas," the employee rationalizes, "because management will not listen."

There is a solution. Always reward the time and energy that an employee spends creating an idea. If you consistently reward the time and energy, the employee will continue to produce ideas. We want ideas. Yes, many ideas will fail. But if we stop producing ideas, we will never create the one idea that will work. By rewarding the time and energy spent creating the idea, you ensure your idea pipeline continues producing.

Create a Better Brainstorming Session

Here are the top most dreaded statements in business:

> *We are having the Christmas party this year in the restaurant downstairs in our building.*[5]
>
> *Can we schedule another conference call?*
>
> *Didn't you back up your computer?*

Can I see you in my office with the HR representative?

The printer is jammed.

I need to speak with you about your expense report.

Let us have a brainstorming session in the conference room at 1 p.m.

Right now, we really only have time to discuss the last statement. Brainstorming sessions have become more tedious than calling customer service for your cell phone plan. We have too many bad habits that do not allow us to have productive or creative sessions. The following ideas are not just for brainstorming sessions. They are for any type of creative process in a team environment.

- *Someone has to lead.* Select a leader for the brainstorming session to keep everyone on track. Brainstorming sessions are not bitch sessions, whine sessions, what-did-you-do-last-weekend sessions, gossip sessions, or did-you-watch-last-night's-episode-of-the-hot-television-show-of-the-moment-that-involves-cops-lawyers-doctors-morticians-crime-scene-investigators-or-convicts-turned-private-investigators. Brainstorming sessions are for creating ideas. A leader will help keep everyone on track.

- *Someone has to record the session.* You can either write every idea down, or record the session. It does not matter. As long as you record every idea—even the bad ideas. You never know which bad idea might blossom into something special.

- *Focus your creative energy.* Brainstorming sessions should take place in short bursts. When the sessions become too long, they drag, and you lose the momentum and energy. Experiment with your sessions. Have everybody run into the session and spend only 15 minutes. If you only create ideas and do not analyze, everyone will become more focused.

- *Change the venue.* Sometimes a different location will add some energy to the session. Have the session in a nearby coffee shop, museum, restaurant, parking lot, ice-cream shop, or your building's lobby. Just get out of the conference room.

- *Be open to suggestions and build on each other's ideas.* One idea will lead to another idea. In a short creative session, you want as many ideas as possible. Help each other. Create a positive environment that encourages idea generation. The result is a more productive, creative, and fun session.

- *Get everyone involved.* If we encourage building on each other's ideas, then we all have a stake. The idea is not owned by one person. The idea is owned by everyone. Buy-in will become easier because everyone has a stake in the ownership of the idea.

- *Try something different.* If you cannot find a new place, try a game. Try food. Sit on the floor. Play music. Give everyone crayons. Creativity detests repetition and doing things the same way.

I hope some of these suggestions will help your innovation. Keep in mind, what works for one person may not work for another. You have to figure out what you need to create. And when you realize what you need, then search for it, fight for it, and demand it.

One of the most rewarding aspects of my job is realizing the creative power we each possess. I am still amazed by the creativity, humor, fun, and energy displayed by the participants who come on stage with me. Some are volunteers. Some are chosen. And some are forced on stage by their peers. I have had participants from practically every industry, from every level of business, and from all across the world. They are all creative.

Have fun. Be creative. Stand up to the creative zombies who think there is only one animal name that starts with the letter Z. Come on, have you never heard of a Zanzibar day gecko or a zigzag salamander?[6]

Quick Ideas

We rarely have time to just think. We run from project to meeting to conference call. And then we go home and run from soccer practice to school to the grocery store to the craft store to pick up something for our child's history report.

- Take five minutes every day for your own think session.

- Leave your phone at your desk and take a walk by yourself.

- Go outside and sit on a bench, or take a seat in the lobby.

- Now, all you have to do is think. You do not have to think about any particular problem or issue. Just relax and think. I am sure you will come up with an idea every time. It might be a small idea or it might be a big one.

If you are a manager, encourage your employees to take a five-minute think session each day. You will see the benefit in the form of ideas. And we all have five minutes to spare. If you do not think you have five minutes because you are too important or too busy, then you should visit a cemetery.

If you must, put a note on your desk that says: "Relax, think, and create."

Chapter 15

Life Happens in the Front Row

Twenty years from now you will be more disappointed by the things you did not do than by the ones you did do. So throw off the bowlines. Sail away from the safe harbor. Catch the trade winds in your sails. Explore. Dream. Discover.

—Mark Twain

This chapter is about risk. One of my favorite activities at an event is watching people walk into the meeting room. I listen to their comments. I watch where they sit. You can tell quite a bit about people by where they choose to sit in a room. The back row people immediately stake out their territory. The front row people move quickly and efficiently. The middle row people sit in one seat, look around, and then move to another seat. And they choose their seats based on their comfort level with risk.

When I have a small group, I like to arrange the chairs in a horse-shoe shape with no tables. There is nowhere to hide. The attendees walk into the room, immediately stop, dart their eyes around the room, and say something like, "Uh-oh, I think we are in trouble now." I hear nervous laughter. They really do not know what to do. Their plans of sitting in the back of the room, working on their laptop, playing the latest game on their phone, or scrolling social media are dashed. The attendees realize they will have to engage. I giggle as I eat my free granola bar.

When I have larger groups, I do not have the luxury of creating a room without a back row. There are really three areas to a room, and attendees choose their seat based on their comfort level with risk exposure. Of course, the risks are relative. This is not about whether they can handle hiking through the Amazon, climbing Mount Everest, swimming with great white sharks, catching a spitting cobra, or eating at a truck-stop diner. The only danger they might face at a typical meeting is the possibility of having to answer a question, listen to the speakers without answering email, or engage in the presentation.

The Front Row

The front row people are my favorite. There are certain companies that are composed only of front row people. You can stand on stage and talk about eating carrots, and they would applaud, walk out of the meeting, and tell people, "Man, I just saw the best speaker in the world. He has a wonderful story about eating carrots. It really motivated me." Front row people are excited and ready to participate. Front row people are your early adopters and superstars.

Front row people are curious, passionate, and excited to attend the meeting. I could hug front row people. You know, when we were kids, we were all front row people. When I speak to high school and college kids, they run into the room and claim the best seats in the front. The students want to engage and take a risk. The students also realize that you cannot participate and engage from the back row and, more importantly, that you cannot see a damn thing from there. They understand that life happens in the front row.

There is one small subset of front row people in the corporate environment. When the key executives sit in the front row to set a good example, there are always feeder fish who want to sit close by. They have one purpose: kissing ass. You know who I am talking about, Kyle.

The Middle Seats

The middle rows may not have the same frenetic energy of the front rows, but they will listen and participate. As a speaker, you have to prove something to the middle rows. If they do not like what they are hearing, they will tune you out. The people in the middle still care. They just want some protective space. Middle row people want proximity to the action in case something exciting happens. And, if nothing exciting happens, they want to sit far enough from the stage that they can close their eyes or check their email.

Middle row people are interested in what is happening. They will participate if asked but will rarely volunteer. If you make the proper effort, middle row people will engage in the activities.

Middle row people are the middle of the bell curve. You have to support and encourage them, motivate them, and provide a foundation for success.

The Back Row

The people sitting in the back of the room are detached and usually do not plan on participating. They are afraid to participate because they are afraid of risk. They aren't really interested in anything new.

I remember one event where the entire audience sat in the back three rows of the room. The front five rows were empty. I wasn't going to waste my time and speak to empty rows. So, I introduced myself and walked to the back of the room. The audience then had two choices: turn their seats around to face the back (which was now the new front), or they could watch an empty stage. They opted to move their chairs. It was one of my finer moments.

Let me pose a question. Would you want your doctor sitting in the back row of a conference? How about your banker or accountant? We have to participate and take risks to become more creative,

Life Happens in the Front Row

effective, productive, and successful. To take risks, we have to get involved. And we cannot do that from the back row.

Pay attention to the back row. The people sitting in the back row are either late or do not want to engage and participate. My guess is that those in the back row are not going to do much to help the team reach their goals and create success.

Where Do You Sit?

Where people sit in the audience is relative to their risk tolerance. Maybe "risk" is the wrong word. Risk-taking is about trying something new. It is about creating change to become happier, more productive, or more effective. Risk is a necessary part of business. Without risk, we stagnate. We become complacent, slow, and old. We lose our ability to learn, grow, and develop. The worst thing anyone could ever say to me is, "This is the way we have always done it." People should be fired for uttering those words. If we lived by these words, we would still be living in caves, hoping that the lightning god strikes a tree to make fire.

We are afraid of risk.[1] Many times, we are afraid of something new. What exactly are we afraid of? We are afraid of failure, looking foolish, or making a mistake. We are afraid to lead. We are afraid to follow. We are afraid someone will think we are stupid. Sometimes, we even have a fear of success. There is no room in improvisation for fear. If you are afraid, you will lack confidence. Those fears increase the stress and pressure and do not allow us to effectively create, communicate, or lead.

The week I am writing this chapter I have seen three partners in an accounting firm come on stage and act as if they were bull riders. Wait, it gets better. How about a top-level executive at a software company imitating a giraffe on stage? Have you ever seen a doctor jump around like a kangaroo? Seriously, it really does not get any better than this. That's my job. And it happens every week. I remember an older vice president of an energy company, wearing a very conservative suit, who had to imitate a fish during an exercise. He flopped around the stage, swam through the audience, and flapped his arms like flippers. He was a fish, and a damn good one. I also remember a very high-powered executive who did the best gymnast impression I have ever seen. Anyway, I get to make people laugh, tell them what I think, and sometimes make them dance like ballerinas. I do not even hypnotize them. And that was just a couple of examples. I am always amazed when the audience participants take risks. And I think they are amazed by their own creativity and the subsequent rewards of applause, laughter, and a sense of accomplishment.

Why do people take a risk and come on stage with me? Is there something we can learn and take back to our teams? Interestingly enough, not everyone who comes on stage is a volunteer. Often, I have to call a name or pick someone from the audience. It is pretty rare that someone refuses to come on stage with me. In fact, I cannot remember the last time someone refused. Remember, I am usually speaking to audiences full of engineers, accountants, information technology professionals, doctors, lawyers, bankers, or people who make concrete pipe.[2] Would you expect any of them to dance like ballerinas? They do. They all do. And I am amazed every time.

By examining why audience members take the risk and come on stage, we can understand how to create the proper environment at our offices. We want people to understand and find a comfort level with change and risk. We want our employees to embrace and develop new ideas, concepts, and ways of doing business.

There are four basic actions I take to create an environment for my audience to feel comfortable enough to take risks. They take no budget and very little time, but they pay huge dividends.

1. *Make the employees feel comfortable*. From the moment I step on stage, I want to create a comfortable and safe environment. I want the audience to understand we are going to have fun, we are going to learn, and, more importantly, we are not going to take ourselves too seriously. How do I do this? I connect with the audience. I speak *to* them and not *at* them. I use the right tone of voice. I choose my words carefully. I pay attention to them.

   It really does not take much to create a comfortable environment. Yes, for most people, taking a risk is difficult. Change is difficult. You may have to learn something new. You might have to change the way you work. You might make a mistake. But if you can make employees feel comfortable and appreciated, they will eagerly take a risk and try something new. A negative environment only builds stress and fear.

2. *Create a positive environment*. Sometimes my clients ask me, "Are you going to make fun of people?" I have to nip that in the bud quickly because they do not understand. Certainly, some people are more involved than others. Still, it is about creating a very positive environment. Every person who comes on stage with me is going to get at least four rounds of applause. I will continuously give them support and positive feedback. They will also receive positive support from the audience's laughter and applause. Each instance of positive support builds their confidence and allows them to take more risks.

   If someone makes a mistake, I patiently correct them. At the same time, I give them positive support and encourage the audience to do the same. The volunteers learn from their mistakes and always move forward in a successful and productive way.

Every moment of improvisation is about taking a risk. However, it is easier to take that risk when you are working in a positive and supportive environment.

When I am at my best, I am not only receiving positive support from the audience but also from my teammates. That support gives me the confidence to create and produce. Without that confidence, I would fail.

3. *Support your teammates as they take risks.* The people who come on stage will make mistakes. I want the volunteers to learn from their mistakes, stay in the game, and find a way to succeed. I am patient with the audience members. I never get frustrated with them. I help them, advise them, and give them the necessary feedback for them to make the right choices.

The audience volunteers also have to work with each other on stage. Sometimes they know each other, and sometimes they do not. I rarely see any frustration or impatience. Yet, in the work environment, we become frustrated and impatient all the time. What is the difference? The audience volunteers playing the improvisation game are having fun. They are more open to each other, more helpful, and more understanding. They understand that they have to work together to achieve success. Again, improvisation forces them to make the right choice in how they work together. If they get frustrated or become unsupportive, the games do not work.

4. *Refrain from judging.* In an earlier chapter, I discussed the "bunny, bunny, bunny" exercise. If you have already forgotten the story: the first thing I do when I speak to an audience is to ask everyone to put their thumbs to their temples, flap their hands, and say, "bunny, bunny, bunny." I took this from an old improvisation warm-up game. Everyone in the audience

147

Life Happens in the Front Row

laughs, even the grumpy people. It is pretty hard to stay grumpy and bitter when someone has their thumbs stuck to their temples and keeps saying, "bunny, bunny, bunny." Tens of thousands of people including CEOs of huge corporations, every level of executive, every level of employee, and people from so many countries that I have lost count have done the "bunny, bunny, bunny." They all laugh. They all giggle. And every single person who does the "bunny, bunny, bunny" looks foolish and silly. Why do they do it? They do it because we supported each other and we did not judge. That is the key to taking a risk.

Go outside and walk up to someone you do not know, and do the "bunny, bunny, bunny." The next time you speak to your customer give him or her a little "bunny, bunny, bunny." You probably would not even attempt it. Why? Because people would think you lost your mind and call the police. Yet, when I ask my audiences to "bunny, bunny, bunny," every person participates. Once in a while I will have one person who will hesitate as the whole audience is doing "bunny, bunny, bunny." I point them out. He or she looks around. The crowd rallies around them and applauds. Guess what. They always end up doing the "bunny, bunny, bunny."

"Bunny, bunny, bunny" is the secret. If we support each other and do not judge, it is easier to take a risk. We will try something new. We will not have a fear of making a mistake or looking foolish because we understand everyone will support us. That support is very powerful. That support will make you dance like a ballerina. And I do not even have to hypnotize you.

Taking a risk is a choice. Risk is about trying something new and stepping out of your comfort zone. It takes courage to be first. It takes courage to step on stage and perform an improvisation game in front of your colleagues. It takes courage to present a new idea or try a new path.

Once you take the first step, you realize your fear is unwarranted. The second step is always easier than the first. The next step is fueled by encouragement and support.

I know you have the courage. I know you can step out of your comfort zone. You just need to take the first step. I promise there will be people to support you.

See you in the front row.

Quick Ideas

The next time you attend a meeting, try one of the following:

1. Stake out a seat in the front row.

2. If you are usually a back row person, try the middle at the next meeting.

3. If you are usually a middle of the audience person, try the front row.

4. Engage with people that are not in your department or region. Find someone new, introduce yourself, and ask a question.

5. Sit at a table with people you do not know, and introduce yourself.

6. When the presenter asks for volunteers, jump out of your seat. Ask questions. Participate.

7. Take the lead in an activity. Be the person who leads the team.

8. Find a new group of people, and go to lunch or grab coffee with them.

---

9. Look for opportunities to participate. At a recent conference, the client had a "story" video booth. You entered the booth and recorded a video answering a question or telling part of your story. It was a new idea. The more people got out of their comfort zone and tried the booth, the more people participated. Be first.

10. Be the person who starts the applause.

Chapter 16

We All Have Choices

The greatest part of our happiness depends on our dispositions, not our circumstances.

—Martha Washington

Happiness depends upon ourselves.

—Aristotle

Improvisation is about choices. You have to make the best choice possible. Since the game does not have a predetermined outcome, there cannot really be an absolutely right or wrong choice. Certainly, some choices are better than others. Some choices are going to lead to a more successful and creative outcome. The key is that each participant has the ability to take ownership and make a choice that gives them the best opportunity for success. How many of us truly take ownership of our choices? Who chooses our attitude? Who makes the choice about our passion and energy at work? Too many times, we allow others to make those choices for us.

Every chapter in this book discusses choices and the responsibility for those choices. When I watch participants play the improvisation games with me, I am amazed by their ability to take ownership of the game. It is not my game. It is our game. When someone comes on stage, they immediately start to care about the objective, the result, and the process. When we have ownership, we care. And when we care about something, we become passionate. Our attitude changes from that of passive observer to that of creative, passionate, energetic participant.

If we can create success with our choices in an improvisation game, why can't we take control of our choices at work? Too often, we give up the choice to be happy, passionate, and energized. We allow our customers, managers, colleagues, partners, vendors, the stock market, the government, and everyone else the option to determine our happiness. When we give up that choice, we are never very happy. How can we be happy? Someone else is choosing our attitude. They do not even know what makes us happy. We have to take responsibility for our happiness and not allow others to make the choice for us. It is our choice.

If it is really our choice, why would any person choose anything but a happy, passionate, and energized work life? Would you wake up in the morning, brush your teeth, and think, "Wow, I am sure pissed off today. I am frustrated, impatient, and stressed out, and I feel great. I am bitter, surly, and angry and I cannot wait to get to my job at International GlobalCom InfoDataVerse Solutions. Yep, this is how I want to walk through the day." Who would make that choice? Yet we see people every day who have made this very choice. Usually, these people work in customer service.[1]

I do not always speak to fun, energetic groups of people. Sometimes I speak to lawyers. I have also spoken to many, many grumpy people. My favorite time to speak is after a question-and-answer period. Nothing gets people grumpier than a question-and-answer period. Everybody gets all riled up because, if there is anything I have learned about the corporate world, is that a question-and-answer period always turns into a feeding frenzy. Eventually, somebody asks the CEO, vice president, or whomever about compensation, benefits, pay raises, or stock options. And then people get really grumpy. Right after that, they introduce me. "Now, we are going to have some fun with Joel . . ."

Side note: I have also followed a segment when the company memorialized a CEO who recently passed. I walked on stage right after the video montage. "Now, let us have some fun with Joel." I have walked on stage right after someone asked for thoughts and prayers for their CEO who was in a coma. "Now, let us have some fun with Joel." How about one more? The CEO walked on stage to announce that the call they were waiting for about their primary customer did not go well. The primary customer would not renew the contract. Two weeks after that announcement, the company was sold off. "Now let us have some fun with Joel."

Back to following the grumpy question-and-answer session: sometimes, it takes an outsider to point out how silly it is to make the "grumpy" choice. Not only is it silly, but we are surprisingly quick to allow something to affect our happiness. I remember one Q&A session where a woman who worked in the company's California office was very upset that she had to travel to the East Coast for a meeting. She was tired. It is a long trip to travel from California to the East Coast, she said. During the Q&A session, she asked why the group could not meet in California. I guess she failed to realize that the corporate headquarters of her company, where we were having the meeting, was on the East Coast. I never did understand her point. But she made the "grumpy" choice. Once a year she had to travel to a meeting on the East Coast, and she was not happy. Why is she so bitter? Does she realize she can get an awesome lobster roll on the East Coast?

We choose to be happy and passionate. And we choose to be annoyed, frustrated, impatient, bitter, and surly. When we choose the latter, our stress levels are higher than the cholesterol in a triple-bacon cheeseburger slobbered with mayonnaise and deep-fried in pork grease.

Choose Your Own Attitude, Not Someone Else's

One of my favorite improvisation games involves three volunteers, each of whom is assigned a different emotion. One of the volunteers is driving a car. As each player enters the car, everyone takes on his or her emotion. When "happy" comes into the car, everyone becomes happy. When "angry" gets into the car, everyone becomes angry. The game is always very funny. Guess which emotion is easiest to express for the players? Yep, it is angry. I have seen every emotion come into the car. Every single time "angry" or "frustrated" comes into the car, the players immediately jump on board. I have seen some volunteers who were very, very good at playing angry. Sometimes, they think they are in therapy.

Why is it so easy to choose the negative emotion? Why do we let negative people influence us? Do we all feel better about ourselves when we can whine in the company of others? How many questions can I ask in this paragraph? Will I ever produce a thought or just keep asking questions? Seriously, when is this going to stop? Why am I asking so many questions? Am I making you upset?

I want to share another story about negative influences and choices. Another exercise, which I have mentioned in a previous chapter, involves 5 to 10 people working together to create a marketing plan for a made-up product. I give them a made-up word such as "MO DU," and as a group they must decide:

- What is a MO DU?

- What are the benefits and features of a MO DU?

- Who is the market for a MO DU?

- How are you going to sell the MO DU?

Finally, each group must create a presentation about their product with a role play or commercial and include an advertising jingle. I give each group about 10 minutes to meet their objective. The limited time forces the group to focus and create and eliminates time for the group to analyze or judge. The group must work together in a positive environment, create support, and build off each other's ideas.

Sometimes, to make a point, I quietly ask one or two people from different groups to be negative during the exercise. No matter what idea is created, they have to shoot it down. Every idea is a bad idea. Yes, I know this is very mischievous.[2]

Here is usually what happens:

- The group with the planted negative person takes more time to meet the objectives.

- The participants in the group with a negative person spend more time trying to appease the negative person than actually working.

- The group with the negative person has less fun.

- The participants in the group with the negative person are generally not as happy with their ideas.

- I have seen people "report" the negative person to me, saying he/she is not playing the game correctly. I have seen groups throw the negative person out of the exercise. I have seen groups ignore the negative person.

- Participants with the negative person are usually more frustrated.

- Sometimes, the negative participants feel bad. They feel so uncomfortable being the negative person that they acquiesce and become positive.

The participants make the choice to allow the negative plant to affect their ability to succeed. The other groups, without a negative person influencing their work, have a more creative, positive, and productive experience. They have chosen to take a more effective path. Everyone is working together on a common objective. More importantly, everyone is involved in the process. They are open to each other's ideas.

On the other hand, I have seen many groups with a negative person overcome the obstacle and create very effective results. Every time I see this happen (and it actually does happen), the group makes the choice to have fun and succeed regardless of the negative person. They make a very quick attempt to involve the person. After that, the group focuses on each other and meeting the objective. They make the choice to stay positive. Can we work this way at our jobs? We spend so much time trying to make the negative people happy that we forget to acknowledge the employees and managers who are creative, do great work, and produce success.

We certainly should reach out to the negative people. After that, they are on their own. Sometimes my clients mention that they have one or two very negative people in their department. They often ask, "How are you going to reach the negative people?" My answer is simple: I do not really care about the negative people. They have made their choice. I would rather spend my energy with the employees and managers who are contributing to success. We spend too much time, energy, and money on employees and managers who have made the negative choice. If everyone else is happy and productive, we are obviously creating the right work environment. I would rather use my resources to encourage the employees who have made the choice to be supportive, positive, and understanding.

The exercise is an amazing microcosm of teamwork. The short time frame and difficult challenge force the participants to make important choices. Each choice allows the group to find success and develop innovative ideas. I am always blown away by the creativity of the groups.

Here are the choices each group makes that lead to success:

1. Each person on the team is valued and treated as equals.

2. Everyone participates in the creative process.

3. Each idea is met with positive support. The positive support entices more ideas.

4. The group encourages each other promoting a positive experience. Everyone is having *fun*.

5. Each participant takes responsibility and ownership, which leads to the group's success.

After each group presents their new product and sings a jingle, I ask an important question. If I gave you an hour instead of 10 minutes, would you create something better? The answer is always no. Sure, the team could spend more time rehearsing their presentation. More time would not produce a better idea. The short time forces the group to make more effective choices:

1. Focus on the task. There is not enough time to wander.

2. Include everyone on the project. The short time forces everyone to participate.

3. The limited time promotes encouragement.

4. Make a creative choice and jump on board. There is not enough time to analyze.

Employees and managers must take ownership of their choices. If we create a positive environment and give each other the right tools, then it is up to each person to make the right choice. Each team member must choose to be open and flexible, to create opportunity and positive support, to be creative, to be an effective leader and communicator. Finally, they have the responsibility to choose to have passion for their work, to be happy, and to be energized.

Although we all have choices, I meet too many people who think they cannot change their situation. Audience members tell me:

- My boss does not promote creativity.

- I do not work in a fun environment.

- My colleagues are negative.

- Our corporate culture is negative.

- I do not have fun at work.

- My manager does not listen to me or communicate very effectively.

These are all difficult situations, and I do not have all the answers. I do know that you will never be happy unless you make certain choices. It only takes one person to begin the process of change. In improvisation, one person saying one line can change the entire outcome of the game. You have to make your own choice. Take ownership and responsibility for your choice. Be happy with your choice.

I do know that if you are at a company that does not give you opportunity and positive support, you may not be at the right place. There is nothing wrong with that fact. I promise there is always another company that will value your passion and innovation. Someone is always looking for a passionate and energized team member that will help build success. Do not settle. Understand that you have value. If your current company refuses to acknowledge your value, then it might be time to find another opportunity.

Make the Right Choice

This is not about being a Pollyanna. Not everything is rosy and happy with woodland creatures dancing around you. Sometimes you have to stand up for yourself. If you take responsibility, you will wake up every morning more passionate, more energized, and happier than you have ever been—because it is your choice.

And the next time you attend a meeting on the East Coast, go find an awesome lobster roll and some wild blueberry pie. I promise your grumpiness will disappear.

Quick Ideas

Take a few minutes to think about the following:

- What is really affecting your ability to be happy, passionate, and energized at work?

- What makes you frustrated and impatient?

- What causes you stress?

Take a hard look at the list. You have identified what is causing you stress. What choices are you going to make to regain ownership of your happiness and passion?

For example, my first job out of college was working for a newspaper in Saginaw, Michigan. I wrote about murders. I had to arrive at work at 6 a.m. I lived in an apartment with practically no furniture. I had no money and was driving a 1987 Chevy Spectrum. I was cold every minute I lived in Michigan. Guess what. I chose my attitude, and I chose happiness.

I was in a tough situation, but I made the decision that I was going to have control. I wasn't going to let my environment or situation determine my happiness. I still had tough and stressful days. Nobody is perfect. Now, though, I have ownership of my

---

happiness. Because I chose my attitude, I became more produc-tive and creative, and I enjoyed my work.

My alternative was to come to work every day and whine about my situation. I knew very quickly that was not going to enable success. If I was going to achieve my goals, I had to control my attitude—no matter what the situation.

Figure out what is causing you stress. Take ownership of your happiness and passion, and realize that you have complete con-trol. Once you identify what is causing you stress and preventing your happiness, it becomes very easy to take responsibility and make the right choices.

Chapter 17

Stand and Be Recognized: A Few Thoughts on Awards and Recognition

Do not worry when you are not recognized, but strive to be worthy of recognition.

—Abraham Lincoln

A ward presentations are boring. There, I said it. Yet nobody will ever stand up and demand that award galas change. We just keep going through the motions, giving out pointy glass awards, and eating our chicken dinners. Managers feel good. The company feels satisfied. The audience wants to jam the salad fork into their thigh to stay awake.[1]

Many of my clients view award presentations as a required obstacle. They just want to get through the process like a colonoscopy. They hit the same beats on the same drum each year.

How did everything get so tired and boring? Where did we go wrong? Award presentations should snap with energy, fun, and festivities. We should celebrate the winners. We should appreciate and thank everyone involved in our success. Most of all, the awards should motivate us to achieve.[2]

What do we do? A vice president, who should never speak in public with a microphone, is allowed to announce a list of winners with the same amount of passion used when reading the ingredients of breakfast cereal. The presentation becomes a long march toward a black hole of emptiness. Sure, we applaud at the right time. We congratulate the winners. And then we drive home and forget the night ever happened. If we are lucky, there is an '80s cover band that crushes Bon Jovi's "You Give Love a Bad Name."

And that is not even the saddest part. This night of nights, against which all other boring nights will be compared, is the only time some of these employees and managers receive any recognition. We put everybody in one room, we eat chicken and rice pilaf, give out a few awards, and that's it. We are done until next year.

We can change. We can grow. We need to do more to recognize our employees and managers. This is more than creating a positive environment. And this is not creating a work environment for third graders where everybody receives recognition no matter what colorful mess they create in art class. This is about making sure you recognize people for their ideas, efforts, and successes. I have a few ideas about recognition and award presentations that are fun, motivating, and exciting. Slowly, put down the salad fork; everything is going to be fine.

First, let us discuss the awards night.

Best Use of Wasted Time: The Photographer

Here's an idea. Let us bring the event to a screeching halt while the photographer takes a picture of everyone standing in a line on stage holding a pointy glass award. Yep, sounds like a winner to me. We should stop the action after every award. Nothing will happen on stage. The energy in the room will remind you of a macroeconomics class on a spring Friday afternoon. And now we have an awesome photo of everyone standing in line on stage holding a pointy glass award.

The solution: have the photographer take as many candid photos as he or she wants during the event. Just do not stop the action for a photo. Instead, ask the award winners and presenters to stay after the program. The photographer can quickly take all of the photos.

Not only are you not stopping the action—you are probably cutting about 15 minutes from the program. Waiting for the photographer to take a photo of people standing in a line holding a pointy glass award are . . . really . . . long . . . minutes.

If you do not want to take photos after the program, create a photo station to the left or right of the stage with a backdrop. Station a second photographer there to take the grip and smile photos. As soon as the award winner walks off stage, they can take a grip and grin photo with their manager, division president, or someone dressed up like a super hero.

Best Recognition of Everyone in the Room

Winning an award is fun. Watching anyone other than your favorite actor/actress/band/solo artist win an award is not fun. It is easy to forget the other employees and managers in the room who are not receiving awards. How exciting do you think the night is for them? Appreciate and involve everyone in the room to create a more festive and interesting evening.

Here's one idea: during dinner, have a PowerPoint presentation running in the background with photos of employees and managers with quick notes on their successes, such as a key sales win or a thank-you quote from a customer. Sprinkle in some fun facts and photos. Attendees will casually read the slides while having dinner and start talking about the presentation.

If you do not think seeing a photo of Doug from accounting climbing Mount Kilimanjaro, Lindsey from HR finishing a marathon, or Garland from the data center in a Civil War uniform reenacting the Battle of Gettysburg is interesting, well, you just aren't living.

Look for other ways to include everyone in the special evening. Create an inclusive event for everyone in the room. Make the night special for the award winners *and* the team.

Best Use of Reading to Inflict Boredom

Edit the script. Sounds simple, yet the award scripts are too long, too repetitive, and too general. Focus on what the team member did to deserve the award and less about the description of the award. Audiences want to hear a story about the winner because it creates a connection. Some of my favorite moments at award shows are when someone is telling a funny or inspirational story about the recipient.

Here is a simple goal for every award event or meeting: read less. The last time people enjoyed someone reading to them was when they were four years old and their father was reading *Harold and the Purple Crayon*.

Speak from the heart. Tell a story. Nobody cares if you forget to say something. If you have to read, rehearse and see whether you can say some of the presentation off the cuff. Too much reading makes people sleepy. Reading the nomination is a great idea. Reading a nomination for each of the 20 awards bores the audience the same way the person at the car dealership trying to sell a paint warranty bores me.

Choose a key paragraph from the nomination letter to read or paraphrase. Create a booklet of the complete letters to hand out at the ceremony or post on the company's internal site.

Instead of reading the nomination, have a manager speak from the heart about the award recipient. Please do not script the award manager. Have faith. As a manager or a vice president, he or she may have occasionally had to put a few words together. Award scripts all sound the same because they are written without feeling. Let the presenters speak from the heart to create a more memorable and entertaining presentation. Yes, they might make a mistake. They might even flub a few words. Does anyone really care?

The only thing less exciting than reading the nomination letter is reading off a long list of names. What do we think happens when someone hears their name read from a list of 35 others? "Honey, I had to call you. Someone read my name off a list because I have worked at the company for five years. I feel so recognized and satisfied."

Save the list for the intranet. Just ask everyone to stand as a group and give them a round of applause.

Best Way to Save the Evening: Hire a Professional

I like Marvin, the vice president of the International Global Sales division. Marvin is a very nice guy. I am not sure I need to listen to him host the awards evening. Marvin does not go to rehearsal. Marvin does not listen when you explain the flow of the evening. Marvin should stick to international global sales.

Why do we not give Marvin a little help? The easiest way to add some fun to an awards presentation is to hire a professional emcee.[3] Like anything, there are good hosts and bad hosts. The good hosts know how to recognize the winners, include the audience, and make the night entertaining. If you have a limited budget, ask your keynote speaker if he or she would also host your award program. Most good speakers make excellent hosts or emcees and will not charge much more if the event is the same day they are speaking.

A professional makes the event run more smoothly. A professional will also transition from one award to the next and handle any production hiccups. Marvin would throw his hands in the air, look blankly into the audience, and ask nobody in particular when he is supposed to give out the next pointy glass award.

It is time to shake up the award presentation. If you have done the same thing for 15 years, it is time to change. Find ways to create excitement and add fun to the evening. You do not have to take every moment so seriously.

Attendees will appreciate any change. A simple adjustment, such as changing the order of the awards during the evening, will refresh a stale presentation. Ask the award winners to say a few words. Some may choose to speak, and some may not. When I have seen the winners say a few words, it is a memorable experience and adds more heart to the evening.

When all else fails, tell Marvin the event is at a different hotel, and hide the salad forks.

Here are a few other ideas for your award presentation:

1. Use video. We are in a video revolution. Audiences are accustomed to low-budget video on social media. Yes, you can hire professionals to create awesome video. You can also create awesome, fun (and cost-effective) videos on your phone to recognize award winners.

2. Take an entertainment break. I had a client hire various performers to entertain during the awards. We would give out a few awards, and then an incredible circus-type act performed for the audience. The client hired four or five different acts to perform in between the awards. It was awesome.

3. Do not take the event too seriously. Have fun. Be creative. Try something new.

4. Have fun. Please see above.

5. Two words: confetti cannon. This is my favorite idea. I had a client who *loved* confetti cannons. The production team would shoot off the cannon after each award. The audience loved it. The photos were spectacular. The hotel hated it. Oh, there is a *big* cleaning fee for confetti cannons. Worth it.

6. Create surprises. My client was having a virtual awards presentation and asked for ideas. I had this idea for a band to

record a song with just the person's name. We would show the custom video after each award. I found an awesome musician who took it even further. The band customized a popular song for each award winner. The client loved it and used the concept several times, including at in-person programs. And the award winner received a video of their "song."

More Ideas for Recognition

Okay, now a few ideas about recognition when we are not eating chicken and rice pilaf and giving out pointy glass awards.

- *Talk about recognition.* Have you ever discussed recognition with your employees or managers? Have a discussion. Discuss what kind of recognition your employees would appreciate. What is important? What is not important? By having a discussion, you are no longer guessing.

- *Remember to show your appreciation.* This really sounds simple, huh? When you are having the discussion about recognition, ask your employees and managers how often someone communicates appreciation for their work. I think you will be surprised.

- *Create a program in which employees recognize their peers.* Do the same with managers. If we want to create a positive environment, it is important to create an environment of respect. Recognition should not come just from the top down. It needs to come from your colleagues sitting to your left and right.

- *Create and use different media to communicate appreciation.* Use websites, email, voicemail, newsletters, lunch programs, and even bulletin boards.[4]

- *Have fun and create new ideas.* Bring an old high school debate trophy to work and present it to an employee or manager as recognition for something serious or silly. The recipient has to award the trophy to someone else sometime that week. And so on. And so on. And so on. It does not have to be a trophy. It can be a stuffed animal, traffic cone, or something that has meaning in the office or makes people giggle.

- *Hold a monthly contest.* Ask employees and managers to submit a presentation, photo, or video that demonstrates appreciation or recognition for helpful, productive, or creative achievement. The contest will produce a creative energy and recognition. And it is fun.

- *Take the time.* We do not have to wait until the annual meeting to give out awards and recognize an employee's creative idea, extra effort, support of a project, leadership, or anything else. We do not have to spend any money to create an environment that promotes recognition. We just have to take the time.

Quick Ideas

This chapter is packed with ideas. I am tapped out. I have nothing left for the Quick Ideas section. Take these ideas and run with them.

Can I have some appreciation? How about some recognition? I would really like a pointy glass award.

Notes

Preface

1. Yes, "fungible" is a real word. I heard someone use it during a presentation. The person who used "fungible" in a sentence was very serious. I had to look the word up. I could tell you the definition, but then I would be enabling you.
2. Here are just a few examples: the Concrete Pipe Association, the Fibre Box Association, the National Association of Pupil Transport. Yep, I think I have hit just about every industry.
3. I packed each chapter with tips and ideas. I also included a "Quick Ideas" section at the end of most chapters. There are four chapters that do not have a "Quick Ideas" section because those chapters are so packed with ideas that it would just be redundant. My editor expressed her concerns that readers would revolt about the four chapters without the section. Please take a deep breath after reading the four chapters without a section and just write in your own "Quick Ideas." This is the interactive portion of this book. TA DA!

Chapter 1

1. A version of this chapter has appeared in various online and internal publications. This version is heart healthy.
2. I did see Siegfried and Roy's magic show in Las Vegas. Sat in the front row. Got to pet a tiger cub. The show was not for me. The audience, however, loved every moment of that show. I respected the performers for knowing and understanding their audience. They did not connect to

me. Yet they connected to the rest of the audience. And that was a huge lesson for me: know your audience.

Chapter 2

1. The closing of the newspaper was not my fault. I had nothing to do with it. When I tell the story, people would often say, "it is probably your fault." This is my official declaration of innocence.
2. I am contractually obligated to mention that the day I got married and the birth of my children are also some of the best days of my life. I would also like to include the Kansas Jayhawks winning the NCAA basketball championships in 2008 and 2022; the Kansas City Chiefs winning the Super Bowl in 2020, 2023, and 2024; and the Kansas City Royals winning the World Series in 1985 and 2015.
3. Yeah, I really cannot explain my thought process on why all this happened. I am trying my best. Just remember, at the time I was a 23-year-old idiot.
4. Choosing your attitude also includes choosing how you spend your severance check. And since I was single, young, and had little debt, I chose to go to Las Vegas and to go skiing.

Chapter 3

1. A version of this chapter has appeared in various online and internal publications. If you knew where to look, you could have read this chapter for free; however, this version smells like spring flowers and is carbon neutral.
2. I mentioned zombies in another chapter. Those zombies are like these zombies, yet slightly different. Look, we all know there are different flavors of zombies. Wait, that came out weird.
3. I am fairly certain I made $2.85 an hour when I started my job in 1982 or 1983. It might have even been less. I was paid under the minimum wage. I have no idea why. When I told this story over the years, I always said I made $2.85 an hour. I am sticking with it.

4. In a later chapter, I will discuss what happens when I plant a negative influence in this game.

5. There are so many ideas in this book about celebrating and creating fun TA DA moments. I should have counted them. Note to editor.

Chapter 4

1. A version of this chapter has appeared in various online and internal publications. If you knew where to look, you could have read this chapter for free. However, this version is more dynamic and wind resistant.

2. Thank you for buying/finding/receiving MY leadership book. Thank you for reading this chapter. Please do not sell this book in your next garage sale.

3. Math is hard.

Chapter 5

1. For the younger generations, the age of potpourri happened in the 1990s. Bowls of dried pieces of various trees and plants, dyed in various pigments, and sometimes scented, would be in every house and business lobby. Why? I have no idea. The bowls would collect dust, not smell, and were not interesting to look at. The age of potpourri gave way to the age of scented candles.

2. I was never in a fraternity. My research is based solely on movies I've seen about college life. I just wanted to be up-front about that.

3. Okay, this analogy doesn't work if you are a smoker. So let me help. Just substitute something disgusting instead of smoking. For instance, if someone was gutting a fish, like a big blue marlin, in an elevator, would you ask him to please stop? Good. Now I have made my point.

Chapter 6

1. As I write this revision, my daughter is 21. Recently, one of her room-mates found this chapter during a Google search. Who knew that this

Notes

potty story would give her embarrassment years later? I knew. It was my diabolical Easter Egg.

2. I am sure some older readers, when they use the restroom, yell, "TA DA!" At some point in our lives, we are just excited everything is still working. Don't worry—we will all get there. I think I have entered this time in my life.

3. I talk about the importance of TA DA in several other chapters. I am not repeating myself. It is just really important.

4. I have never—nor will ever—start the wave. I despise the wave. I do not even remember liking the wave when I was a kid. When I am elected Caesar of the Empire, I will ban the wave. All hail Caesar Joel, the great leader who rid our empire of the wave.

Chapter 8

1. A version of this chapter has appeared in various online and internal publications. If you knew where to look, you could have read this chapter for free; however, this version gets better gas mileage and meets most state regulations.

2. This seems like a completely normal road trip through Arkansas.

3. This is next level improvisation. Their action energized me. And the audience saw a magical improvisational moment.

4. I am sure this is the first business book in history that has discussed imitating a giant rat and relieving oneself at the back of an abandoned gas station in Arkansas. And I proudly wear that badge.

Chapter 10

1. In an earlier version of this book, I called the lectern a podium. Someone corrected me on the definition of a lectern and a podium. The lectern is the thing you stand behind. The podium is the stage. I hope the person who corrected me purchases this revised edition, carries the book around, and shouts from the mountain, "I was right!"

2. I have copiously used the word "lectern." And now I have used the word "copiously" in a sentence. Big day.

3. Meeting tip: don't ever show your knees on stage in a Roman tunic. You can never win.

4. This is absolutely a true story.

Chapter 11

1. You are just going to have to take my word that this happened. I could provide statistics and survey results, but that seems like quite a bit of work. Probably 95% of the people who bought this book will agree that this is acceptable.

Chapter 12

1. As I revise this chapter, I just answered an email to schedule a Zoom call with a client. There are 13 other people on the call (this is not a joke). The organizer sent an email to vote on the time. All the times did not work with my schedule. I am hoping the call is scheduled before the next revision of this book. And you know you are in trouble when you are voting for the time to hold the call.

2. Yes, I know there are a plethora of scheduling apps for all of this. Even with the scheduling apps, this still seems to be the process for most of my calls. If you do not believe me, let's schedule a call to discuss.

3. I debated making this joke about *Road House* because I did not want to date the book. Then I considered the following facts: the movie premiered in 1989, we still talk about *Road House*, the movie is always streaming, and it might be the greatest movie ever made.

Chapter 13

1. Part of this chapter first appeared in an article I wrote for *Vision* magazine. Since most of you are probably not members of the California Association of Community Managers, I thought you might enjoy a new and improved version. I do want to thank the editors of *Vision* for giving me the opportunity to write the original article.

2. Okay, I am sorry I had to yell. I wanted to make sure you were listening. I won't yell again.
3. It happened again. Were you listening?

Chapter 14

1. This is an excellent game to play with your children on a road trip. Strangely enough, it is also an excellent drinking game. But I highly recommend that you do not play the drinking game during a road trip with your children.
2. My daughter is now an adult. She has not decreed herself as the abominable snowman in years. I hope her friends read this, and ask about her abominable snowman phase. They should also ask about her octopus, Disney Princess, Harry Potter, and Twilight phases.
3. I realized early on that when I explained any improvisation or interactive exercise, most clients had hesitation. Even now, I read this paragraph and think, "This sounds nuts." Sometimes, you just need to trust me.
4. And for extra value, here are the three most misspelled words when I play this game: gnat, orangutan, and pterodactyl. Please use this information only for good and not evil.
5. This happened to me. I don't really remember how the company announced the holiday party or the general reaction. And I have nothing against the restaurant in the building. It was a fine place for a hamburger at lunch. I worked for a big enough company to have a holiday party. And nothing says, "Please come to our half-assed holiday event that we are obligated to have," more than having the party in the hamburger restaurant in the same building as the office. Obviously, I am still bitter.
6. Both of these animals exist. You can look them up. I did.

Chapter 15

1. It's important to define risk. I am not talking about risks that involve your health and well-being. I am not talking about jumping out of an airplane,

Notes

wrestling a bear with your bare hands, or climbing a mountain. For those in health care, I am not talking about taking a risky course of action. I am talking about business and the risk of change—taking a risk to be more effective, more productive, and happier in conducting business. I just wanted to be clear about risk.

2. Yes, I have spoken to people who make concrete pipe. Actually, I spoke to them very early in my career. The concrete pipe people did not seem to laugh very much. They were very nice but very quiet. Either they were all thinking about making concrete pipe and not paying attention to my show, or they just did not like me. After my presentation, a gentleman approached me and said, "We have not laughed like that in a long time." And I never judged an audience again.

Chapter 16

1. The day I wrote this I had to call my health insurance provider about a billing question. As soon as the customer service person answered the phone, I knew I was in trouble. I could hear her lack of helpfulness in her voice. Usually, I just hang up and call back, hoping to reach someone helpful. This time, I figured I would give her a shot. Nope. She was not happy. After she rushed me off the phone with incorrect and unhelpful information, I called back. I could immediately tell from the tone of the new customer service person's voice that she was going to be helpful in answering my questions. I even told the helpful customer service person about my experience. She said they were all busy. Aren't we all busy? Does anyone have only one thing to do during the day? Let me get this straight. If you work in customer service and you are busy, being friendly and helpful is optional. Huh. Good to know.

2. I am pretty sure I have never written the word "mischievous" in my life. I am excited that I am using the word right now. I kind of feel mischievous. Wow, I did it again!

Chapter 17

1. Please do not do this. It would hurt.
2. Part of this chapter first appeared in an article I wrote for the magazine, *Convene*. Since most of you are probably not members of the Professional Convention Management Association, I thought you might enjoy a new and improved version. I do want to thank the editors of *Convene* for giving me the opportunity to write the original article.
3. This may seem like an obvious plug to hire me as your award night emcee. Just hire a fun professional emcee. And if it happens to be me, well, then I guess this is an obvious plug.
4. I do not remember the last time I checked a bulletin board. I just wanted to make sure I covered every generation. Somewhere out there is a company still using landline phones and posting notices on a bulletin board.

Acknowledgments and a Huge TA DA

1. Every manager should be like Adilson. Books make great gifts. Gifting my book is the gift that keeps on giving.

Acknowledgments and a Huge TA DA

We have fresh wild Atlantic salmon tonight. Do you think any book in the history of publishing has ever started the acknowledgments with the declaration of the catch of the day? Nobody really pays attention to this part of the book. And nobody listens to the waiter recite the chef's specials. Every person at the table is reading the menu or chatting until the waiter says, "We have fresh wild Atlantic salmon tonight."

Pretend we have fresh wild Atlantic salmon tonight.

There are many people I wish to thank for their help, support, advice, friendship, and guidance.

You are reading this revised and expanded edition because of my clients Petrwska Nicholson and Adilson De Andrade, who work at Cinemark. This edition (with the new cover, new subhead, and new and revised chapters) exists because Adilson wanted to purchase copies of this book as gifts for his team.[1] And Petrwska is one of those amazing people who just gets things done.

Petrwska asked to purchase 120 copies. I explained there were production issues and I needed to contact the publisher. And that note sat on my to-do list for some time. The universe and Petrwska had other plans, and the two began working and conspiring together. Petrwska gently nudged me about the books. I promised her I would see what I could do. I emailed my contact at Wiley and explained the situation. Honestly, I expected Wiley to explain that it would not be possible to print more books. That is not what happened. Immediately, Wiley created a timeline to get the copies to Cinemark.

And then the universe stepped in again.

"Would you consider doing a revised and expanded edition of *Make the Right Choice?*" asked the editor at Wiley. I have always wanted to write a new book. I even wrote an outline. That idea and outline sat idle.

The universe was waiting for the right time. This conversation about an expanded and revised edition happened at this time because of Petrwska and her request for 120 books. Huge TA DA to Petrwska, Adilson, and the entire Cinemark team.

And a huge TA DA to Shannon Vargo at Wiley. I emailed Shannon about printing copies of the book for Cinemark. And then we started a discussion about revising and expanding *Make the Right Choice*. Thank you, Shannon.

Huge TA DA to my current Wiley team of Zachary Schisgal, Amanda Pyne, Adaobi Obi Tulton, and Sangeetha Suresh for all of their support, expertise, advice, words of encouragement, and positive energy toward creating the revised and expanded edition. You are holding this amazing love letter to my speaking career because of them. They are also experts in cajoling, pleading, tricking, goading, and manipulating me to adhere to my deadlines. Full disclosure: I never met one of my deadlines.

Writing is a solitary work experience. You write and hope something decent finds a way to the screen and then to a page. I sent in the first chapters to Adaobi. Her reply fueled my work. Her words of encouragement energized me to write and stay on task. Positive support and appreciation are gifts, and Adaobi gave me a truly special one. Huge TA DA!

I also need to thank and give a Huge TA DA to Laurie Harting, my first editor at Wiley. During her research, she found my website. Laurie called me one day and asked why I didn't have a book. We had never spoken, so her call was quite unexpected. I told her, "Because I was waiting for you to call." At least, that is how I remember the story. And for some reason, she still wanted to work with me.

This book would not exist right now without Laurie. I would still be procrastinating and telling people I was planning to write a book. She is a wonderful editor. Her advice, thoughts, and ideas helped me tremendously. I appreciate all of her efforts and hard work and am very fortunate that she was my first editor.

I also want to thank and give a Huge TA DA to Brian Neill and Micheline Frederick at Wiley. I really appreciate all their efforts to make the first edition of this book a reality. I also want to thank Laurie, Brian, and Micheline for bribing, begging, cajoling, pleading, tricking, goading, and manipulating me to meet my first deadlines. I also missed all of those deadlines.

Again, there is wild Atlantic salmon tonight.

Huge TA DA to every performer at Ad-Libs Improvisational Comedy Troupe in Dallas, Texas. When I moved to Dallas in 1991, my friends took me to Ad-Libs for the first time. I was an audience volunteer during one of the games in the show. That night introduced me to improvisation comedy for the first time and changed my life. I joined the troupe in 1993 and found a stage. Every performer that I shared the stage with taught me improvisation comedy.

I performed with some of the most talented improvisation comedians in the country at Ad-Libs. The performers are some of the funniest, most creative people I have ever met. I learned something about comedy and improvisation during every performance. I want to thank all of you for your friendship, support, and inspiration. Most of all, I want to thank you for the improvisation lessons. I don't think I could find better teachers.

I always say I started my speaking career in 1997. I spoke at a few events before 1997. Through the years, I have keynoted or emceed at more than 2,500 events. I want to thank each client, company,

Acknowledgments and a Huge TA DA

organization, association, committee, and board member that said, "We need Joel Zeff at our event." You have given me the opportunity to share my passion. My wife tells our friends that I only want to do two things in life: make people laugh and tell people what I think. My clients give me the opportunity to do both, and I am very thankful and appreciative.

Huge TA DA to every audience member for giving me their most precious gift: their time. We each have a finite amount of time. It is the only item in this world that we cannot buy, steal, beg, borrow, or receive more of during our life. Once we use our time, it is gone. You give me your time, and I appreciate every moment. Each laugh, each round of applause, and each word of appreciation are precious gifts that I treasure.

Huge TA DA to all the people who recommend me to their company, organization, and association. My speaking business happens because a spouse, colleague, friend, executive, manager, friend of a friend, person at a different company, or someone you worked with five years ago saw me speak at a conference. It is true magic how I find my way from one event to the next. Remember the story of how this book happened because of my Cinemark client? An awesome person at Cinemark saw me speak at a conference for Crunchtime, a software company. An awesome person at Crunchtime saw me speak at a conference for the Council of Hotel and Restaurant Trainers (CHART). This is magic, and I appreciate every person that makes it happen.

Huge TA DA to all of the teachers in my life with the exception of every math teacher I had past the sixth grade. I certainly would not be where I am today without my teachers. However, I have no use for long division, algebra, geometry, or even complicated fractions. You were wrong. I did not need to know math.

Finally, I want to thank my family. My children, Isabella and Zander, are my teachers now. Isabella and Zander teach me something

Acknowledgments and a Huge TA DA

every day, and they do not require me to learn math. My wife, Susan, is my best friend, confidante, and partner. She is also an awesome editor. I cherish her support, wisdom, and strength. You help me make the right choices in life.

Take care, and continued success. I hope you enjoyed the wild Atlantic salmon.

J.Z.

About the Author

Joel Zeff creates energy. He is a dynamic keynote speaker, emcee, work culture expert, improvisational humorist, and author. His interactive performances invite members of the audience to participate in hilarious improvisational exercises that illustrate Joel's central message: organizations and individuals should *celebrate* their successes to increase collaboration, productivity, passion, and innovation.

Since 1997, Joel has inspired audiences from Wells Fargo to Samsung to KPMG and even the IRS. Yes, the IRS. Joel is a masterful keynote speaker and a nationally renowned motivator, humorist, and improvisational actor. His spontaneous humor and vital messages have thrilled audiences for more than 25 years, and he has shared his insight at more than 2,500 events.

His career is a search for fun and passion. He quickly realized the importance of both at his first jobs delivering the hometown newspaper and cleaning up trash at a suburban movie theater.

He started his professional career as a newspaper journalist and public relations executive. In 1994, Joel went out on his own as a corporate communications specialist. He helped clients with their internal communications, media relations, strategy, and customer marketing. Throughout the consulting process, Joel realized his clients—many of them high-level technology and telecommunications firms—needed more than marketing and public relations strategy. Many of his clients' employees were starving for fun, passion, and a new perspective on finding success.

At the time, Joel was having fun on the weekends as a comedian. Through friends, he discovered improvisational comedy. One of his clients (a large technology company) knew Joel performed comedy on the weekends. The client invited him to entertain and speak to a group of executives before dinner. A corporate speaking career was born.

He connects to his audience with humor that has them laughing so uncontrollably that their mascara runs, their cheeks hurt, and their bellies ache. And he does not do it alone. Volunteers from the audience join him on stage and play an integral role in an improvisation game in front of hundreds or thousands of people—something the audience members have never done. He expects nothing less than success. He expects the volunteers to focus and work together as a team, communicate effectively, positively support each other, and take responsibility.

Joel makes his audience laugh so hard that they forget about the corporate nonsense of conference calls, "strategic deliverables," PowerPoint presentations with upside-down triangles, or "paradigm shifts in a cross-functional organization." Joel will make you laugh, and he will make you think. His keynotes deliver a combination of inspiration, essential business knowledge, and significant ideas to help audience members reconnect with their own passion and success.

As discussed in his book, *Make the Right Choice*, Joel believes that we all encounter choices in our careers. We always can have the opportunity to make the right choice to live a more creative, passionate, and productive life. How do you make the right choice? You can choose to provide opportunity. You can choose to provide positive support. And along the way, you can choose to have fun.

He has appeared on CNBC and has been featured in the *Dallas Morning News*, the *Houston Chronicle*, the *Kansas City Star*, and many other media outlets. He is attempting to appear on every career, motivation, and/or work culture podcast. He also really likes iced tea.

For more information visit his website at www.joelzeff.com.

About the Author

Index

186

Index

187